WHAT IS GOD SAYING?

HEARING HIS VOICE DURING THE PANDEMIC

MELPHON MAYAKA

urbanpress

What Is God Saying?
by Melphon Mayaka

ISBN 978-1-63360-187-1

For Worldwide Distribution
Printed in the U.S.A.

Urban Press
P.O. Box 8881
Pittsburgh, PA 15221-0881
412.646.2780

TABLE OF CONTENTS

INTRODUCTION

In this Introduction, I state my position as to why I am writing clearly and succinctly. I will add bits of my biography so you also understand where I'm coming from. Every writer writes from the position of his or her biases. This may have to do with the underpinning of their life philosophy, values system, and beliefs, or even the perceived identity of the writer. All those things combine to create a worldview through which the author interprets the world, what is wrong with it, and how it can be fixed. I was taught that one has to make the statement to his position at the outset of a task—I feel I should do the same for my book.

First and foremost, I am a Bible-believing Christian. I believe the Bible is the final authority for Christian belief. It's the final authority in all ethical matters. What's more, I have an African identity. These two concepts will emerge in the book because they shaped and continue to shape how I think—and how I write.

I begin with the story of my earliest upbringing. I was born on November 3, 1963, the second in a family of nine children. I was born into a polygamous family. My father had five wives. Other than my mother, there were four other mothers. So I have many more brothers and sisters, other than the nine, from other mothers. I will use the term brother and sister in this context. I was born in a rural area in Kenya.

Let me begin by explaining my name, Melphon. When I was born in the county hospital, the midwife was Australian. In the fifties and sixties, there were Victorian nurses and midwives who left the state of Victoria in Australia and came to different parts of Africa as missionaries, serving the people in their vocations as health workers. The midwife had the desire to name me Melbourne which is where she came from, but for some strange reason, my parents didn't get the spelling and pronunciation right, so I got the name Melphon.

I remember walking barefoot to a local primary school in the rural area and how painful it was. It would rain sometimes on the way which made it difficult to walk. Sometimes I couldn't get to school. I would instead return home because of the treacherous footing and anticipated long walk without shoes. For reasons unknown to me to this day, we weren't supposed to wear shoes. Only one student had shoes, the school bell ringer, who wore plastic shoes locally known pejoratively in my mother tongue, Ekegusii, as *moiyeki*. I'm not sure why this student was allowed to wear shoes to school while the rest of us were not. I went to the local school until 1973 when I was ten years old.

My father had a positive view of education. He always encouraged his children to get a good education, perhaps because of the exposure he had working as a clerk at a tea plantation in a place called Kaisugu in Kericho County. He later became a local chief. This is a different type of chieftain than those found in other parts of Africa and the world. Those chiefs were appointees of the government, at first the colonial British government, but thereafter the independent Kenyan government. The administrative jurisdiction of the chief was and still remains a location. In hierarchical terms there was a district, then a division, and then a location. The location was headed by a chief.

In the quest to have me obtain a good education, in 1973 my parents decided to send me to a town called Kisii. The aim was to have me live with my sister there in order to get a better education than what I was getting in the local area. So I moved to Kisii Primary School, about 16 kilometers or ten miles away from home. This means I had to be away from my mother, father, and siblings while I stayed with sister, who was the eldest child in the Mayaka family.

I lived with her from 1973 through 1976 and then in 1977, when again in the interest of me getting an even better education, I was moved to a boarding school named St. Mary's Primary School–Mosocho for one year. This was a high performance primary school, not very far from our home. Most of the Mayaka boys went through the school beginning with the late Joseph James Oyaro Mayaka. Going through St. Mary's became a rite of passage of sorts, a tradition to the extent that some Mayaka grandchildren have passed through it. When I joined the school, the goal was for me to do well in the Kenya Certificate of Primary Education (KCPE), which I did, having scored 32—four points short of the highest possible score of 36.

Next door to the primary school was a sister high school and the expected destination of most of the students graduating from St. Mary's. The name is Cardinal Otunga High School–Mosocho. However, while my classmates who performed well joined Cardinal Otunga, I ended up in Maseno National School in another district. The headmaster at St. Mary's, Brother Labert Nissink (now deceased), was quite disappointed that I was selected to another school instead of Cardinal Otunga like the rest of my classmates. He was not amused! Unbeknown to me, this "missed opportunity" or "misfortune" occurred due to a complicated selection system that determines who attends which school. Suffice it to say that I ended up going to another school for my high school education. It is there that I got what's called Ordinary or "O level" education. I also took my two-year advanced or "A level" education in Maseno.

In Maseno, I became a Cubicle Boy, someone who had a little bit of privilege, as a helper to the prefect. I didn't have to do the normal manual labor the other students did. I also got to eat and have better food in the Cubicle. In my second year, I was assigned to work in the dispensary and handle medicine. I had a supply of anti-malarial tablets and would bring them to the dormitory to distribute to my fellow students. We were required to take that to protect ourselves against malaria.

That again afforded me a bit of privilege since I was exempted from having to do some manual duties like the rest of the students. I went on to become a senior dispenser. That meant I was a leader of all the dispensers in all the dormitories. That also meant I lived within boarding facilities in the dispensers and not in the dormitories with the other students.

The reason I give you all that background is that I had a childhood dream of being a doctor. As I progressed in my education, I took subjects that would predispose me toward a degree in medicine, and that included classes in physics, chemistry, and biology. My aim was to become a doctor. I even earned the nickname "Doc" from my fellow students.

Even with that background and with my drive and determination (as well as my nickname Doc), in my final exam in 1983 I did not get good enough grades to join university, let alone go into medicine. I was frustrated and felt like a failure. At that time, when anyone failed that exam, it was pretty much the end of them ever going to a university. I then had to look to vocational education training (VET) , the only option for those who could not go on and join university.

It was at that point I left my rural home in 1984 to live with one of my many brothers in Nairobi, the capital of Kenya. That same year, I accepted the Lord Jesus Christ as my personal Savior. Later that year in October I was to join Kenya Utalii College, a VET institution that trained people for the tourism and hospitality industry. I gained admission to pursue a tour guiding and administration course of study, a two-year program.

In 1985, I was appointed the Christian Union chairperson at the school, the leader of the Christian Union. At that time, the Christian Union was a significant movement in Kenya. It saw Christians from different denominations gathering together on college and university campuses. We would hold meetings, invite speakers, and sometimes have services on Sunday for people who, for whatever reason, could not leave the campus to go to church elsewhere.

In college I was a good student, particularly good in the German and French languages. I found I had a good inclination towards learning languages. I was designated to go to Germany to further my language training and get a scholarship, but that never happened for one reason or another.

After two years, I graduated and went to work for a tour firm as their meet-and-greet person, meeting clients at the airport and at hotels. By the time I left the company, I held the position of deputy operations manager. During that time, I was serving at the Kenya Assemblies of God in the Buruburu area of Nairobi, which is where I got saved.

Alongside my tourism work, I became the youth leader

and the chairman of the youth group in the church. I wasn't considered the youth pastor but with what I did as the youth leader, it was almost like being the youth pastor. I served as the youth leader for a number of years, from late 1987 to about 1992. I would lead overnight prayer meetings and we would hold other meetings, rallies, and youth camps. We had a team of youth leaders and I was their head for that period.

In 1990, while I was working, an opportunity arose for me to be a tutor in the college where I had studied, Kenya Utalii College. I applied and got that position and so joined Kenya Utalii College as a tutor. Then I completed some certificate courses to help me be a better teacher. In 1993 I got a scholarship opportunity to earn a degree as part of a transfer credit, so off I went to the U.S. to Columbia College in Columbia, Missouri. I was there for one year and received a Bachelor of Arts degree. It only took one year because of my credits that they accepted toward the degree. In 1994, I went back to Kenya Utalii College. I met my dear wife Esther there and we got married on July 8, 1995.

In 1997, I received a merit scholarship which is how I got to Australia to attend Griffith University in Queensland. Later, I moved to Victoria University, and guess what happened? I, Melphon, whose name was meant to be Melbourne, landed in Melbourne in March of 1998 where I studied at Victoria University of Technology. I had left my wife and child back in Kenya but in the middle of 1997, they joined me in Queensland. My son was only six months old when they came to Australia. On January 26, 1999, we celebrated our second born whose name is Joshua Omingo. January 26 is called Australia Day. Then Isaac, the last born was born June 2, 2002. I graduated from Victoria University of Technology (now just Victoria University) with a master's degree in business in tourism management.

In September 2002, I returned to Kenya with my wife and three children. I worked in a restaurant for nine months on a temporary basis as a manager on consultancy basis. Then I got a position as a lecturer at Moi University in Eldoret, about 300 kilometers away from Nairobi. From 2003 to 2005, I commuted to Eldoret from Nairobi which wasn't easy. During that time, I developed a very serious back problem and had to take painkillers every day. The pills had an effect for eight hours but after eight hours I reverted to excruciating pain. Then one day my family decided we could not continue that. They decided to join hands and pray for me, God was gracious and healed me. I was healed and have never had a back problem since.

While I was working in Eldoret in 2003, a tragic thing happened. I lost my mom (my father had died in 1985). It was a devastating blow to me. My sisters were married so I was left with the responsibility of being a parent according to Kenyan culture. All my siblings looked to me when they needed help. That wasn't easy.

In 2005, I joined Kenyatta University, Kenya's second-largest university. I had a very good career there. One of the highlights was that I was a pioneer and founding chairman of the Department of Tourism. Along with that, I had a hand in the formation of the School of Hospitality and Tourism. While there, I was also appointed to the board of elders at Kenya Assemblies of God Church in Buruburu, my home church. That was the only church I had known since coming to Jesus. I also served in the men's fellowship which I had helped to establish.

I say all this because I like to create and innovate things. If I see a need, I I feel the drive to create a solution. God has graced me this way. One such entity I helped create is a couple's fellowship at KAG Buruburu (now East Assembly), called Marriage Care Ministry. That was quite fulfilling because my wife and I began that ministry together. I served on the board at East Assembly from 2003 to 2010.

In 2010, we clearly felt God was moving us to something else. At that time, I had the urge to complete my doctor of philosophy, Ph.D. I was teaching at the time but there were things happening that made my attempts to do it locally very challenging. One of the things that happened was that my laptop was stolen that had the Ph.D. proposal in it. That was devastating as I had to shelve my Ph.D. plans for a while. Other doors were also closing before me.

Then one day in June 2009, I applied for a scholarship in Australia, although this wasn't part of my plans. We actually had said we would never go back to Australia. My family and I had plans we wanted to see succeed in Kenya. For example, my wife is a qualified and certified chef and had a café business she had established. She's a genius in terms of food. By the way, I believe in prayer so I prayed God would send me a wife who knew how to cook. God heard my prayer, for she is a great cook—as well as a great person, friend, and wife! She's a perfect companion.

As God would have it, I got a scholarship to study at Monash University in Australia. I applied for the visa and it was declined multiple times, but was finally approved on the fourth attempt after I had actually given up on making any other application. Incidentally, there had been a prophecy when we left earlier that we would come back to Australia, but we never really wanted to come back. Our pastor then, Pastor Philip Hills of Richmond Assembly of God (now Neuma Church in Melbourne), prayed at the time of departure from Australia. He prophesied and prayed that we would return but we didn't think it would happen and never paid attention to the prophecy until it came to pass.

I arrived back in Australia in 2011 but had once again come without my family. The plan was for me to return since I had a successful career in Kenya, and there were hopes and dreams that I would rise within the ranks in the university to university vice chancellor. I had mastered the university system and was doing well as an academic, doing the right things in terms of progress in research and teaching. I remember one of my former masters students asking me to finish my Ph.D. studies quickly and then come back and supervise hers as well. I had a very good rapport with my boss, the Kenyatta University Vice Chancellor, Professor Olive Mugenda, who believed in me so much that the idea of having a school of hospitality and tourism was birthed as a result of a meeting I had with her one day.

Then I came to Australia but my family did not join me. It wasn't easy for us to be separated geographically that way.

In December 2011, I traveled back to see them and then my research took me back home for five months from the end of 2012 to March 2013. Through prayer and seeking God, my wife and I felt they needed to join me. She particularly prayed, saying, "If this [moving to Australia] is for real, I want it to go fast. I don't want to have to wait for the visa the way my husband did, Lord." Thankfully God heard her prayer and her visa process went quickly. She also got the children's visas and they all joined me on April 22, 2013. We've lived ever since in Melbourne.

Let me back up a little. In 2001, we formed an organization or a fellowship called KenAus Fellowship. Under its banner, we wanted to bring people together for prayer, fellowship, and worship but then it disbanded. After we came back to Australia in 2014, we reestablished the KenAus Fellowship with a few friends. I am happy to report that today it is incorporated in Australia and we have seen good results from that effort. KenAus Fellowship brings people together from different denominations and serves as a way for Kenyans in Australia to connect. More on that later.

In 2014, a friend invited me to be an assistant pastor in his church, True Light Christian Church. It was about 45 kilometers from where we lived but every Sunday and for weekly meetings my family and I would be there. In August 2016, we planted a church called Uwezo Liberty Church in one of the suburbs of Melbourne where I am now the senior or lead pastor.

My wife also serves as a pastor. My son Elijah plays drums, my son Joshua leads services and worship and is a guitarist, and Isaac is a keyboard player. Melphon has founded a church in Melbourne. This is where we feel God has called us. That's important because we feel God has given us a mantle of leadership to provide mentoring for younger people in particular.

Our mission statement found on our website is "to enable every individual to have a meaningful relationship with God and with others in order to be who God wants them be so they may accomplish God's purpose for their lives on earth." Our motto is "to be all God wants us to be." We feel called to help and guide people to discover and pursue purpose so they can serve God in different locations and through different callings and areas of expertise.

No one who has lived through the COVID-19 pandemic will ever forget it and how it challenged many things we had come to take for granted, things like church attendance, meetings, relationships, or family gatherings. What God is saying through the pandemic and aftermath is an important question. Many people have their own ideas, including this writer. God is always speaking to His people. He wants His people to hear His voice and know His will. This time of the crisis of the Coronavirus pandemic was no different. We have sought and continue to seek the voice of God because His perspective is eternal or rather has eternal consequences.

This is the essence of the gift of prophecy. A prophet is a mouthpiece for what God is saying. The gift of prophecy brings God's voice to His people and the situations in which they find themselves. Prophecy brings the revelation of God's knowledge and wisdom so His people can gain understanding of His will and purpose. In so doing, they can respond and live, hopefully, the way God wants them and in a manner that is pleasing to Him and in ways that bear fruit for His kingdom (see Colossians 1:9-10).

God's kingdom is all about what He is doing, what He wants to accomplish eternally, as He has been doing since Creation and the Fall. Matthew also referred to it is the Kingdom of Heaven in his gospel. The prophetic voice reveals the Kingdom purpose since God does nothing without revealing His secrets to His servants: "Indeed, the Sovereign Lord never does anything until he reveals his plans to his servants the prophets" (Amos 3:7). As was in the beginning at creation, God does things through His word, meaning He speaks and it happens. A lot of what He is doing He Has already spoken or revealed through His servants. In this book, therefore, I aim to bring understanding of what is happening and, more importantly, what God is saying to us prophetically through the examination of the Scriptures.

I felt the need and urge to write in the context of the

Coronavirus pandemic because the situation was unprecedented. There were several prominent conspiracy theories that actually circled the globe. The crisis brought the entire world to a halt and there were millions of deaths, national lock-downs, and a growing worldwide economic crisis that as I write is still playing out in various parts of the world. I read on Wikipedia that the Spanish Flu, the "deadliest in history, infected an estimated 500 million people worldwide—about one-third of the planet's population—and killed an estimated 20 million to 50 million victims, including some 675,000 Americans."

Yet the Coronavirus situation is quite different from what happened in 1918. Since the Spanish flu pandemic, knowledge has increased, and information dissemination through technology connected the world with speedy access to information as was predicted in the Bible (see Daniel 12:4). For this reason, we know much more than people would have known in 1918 during that outbreak.

It's also important to note that the information access is not a privilege of a powerful or elite few since many people now have access no matter where they live. Also, it is by God's hand and Providence that the nations had greater understanding of disease, government, and political systems, economic systems, health systems, and the like. It's interesting, however, that this increase in knowledge did not create greater confidence and hope but instead helped create fear and panic, particularly as these systems seemed to be under unprecedented pressure and attack.

As the Church of Christ, we may at this time be tempted to ask, "Where was or is God when this was or is all happening?" Even the Church seems helpless and vulnerable when things felt like they were spinning out of control during the pandemic. I had to remind myself and reassure my flock that God is still on His throne and that He is the Lord strong and mighty (see Psalms 24:8; 97:1).

Moreover, our help is from the Lord, who made heaven and earth (see Psalms 124:8). This was and is not time to fear but a time to put our trust fully in God. He will save and deliver us when we are in the worst trouble. Even if we die, we will be with Him in Heaven eternally. Fear and terror are not from God, but He allows things to happen and then gives us the freedom to choose our response. We saw some fear and arrogance during the pandemic and our leadership was tested and often found wanting, lacking perspective, insight, or a word for the way forward.

This book is about what God is saying through the pandemic period and the season His people are passing through because He has not stopped speaking! Let's hear what the Spirit is saying to us and the Church.

Melphon Mayaka
Melbourne, Australia
March 2022

1

DISTRESSED BUT NOT DISTRACTED

In the context and aftermath of the pandemic, we can conclude that we are living in unprecedented and difficult times that have brought great amounts of distress to individuals, families, and nations. This led to me to teach and deliver a message titled "Distressed but not Distracted." We were all distressed during the pandemic and that stress caused many leaders and believers to be distracted from the work of the Church and the work God called individuals working in and out of the Church to do.

To say that people are distressed at this moment is a drastic understatement. We are living in challenging times that have brought great distress to individuals, families, institutions, and even nations. People the world over are upset by the interruptions to their lives and the way the response to the pandemic has been or is being handled by those who are at the highest levels of government or church. The world seemed to be spinning out of control.

How did we handle this within the Church? How should we have handled it? What should we have said and what will we say if anything like it ever happens again? Those are all questions that will be discussed (I hope) for years to come and leadership must lead the DMin and apply the lessons to their own work and walk with God.

Yet we can be distressed but we must not be distracted as we look to God. The dictionary defines distress as the process of diverting attention of an individual or group from a desired area of focus, thereby blocking or diminishing the reception of desired information. A critical question for us as God's people is how we move forward from the current situation without being distracted from purpose and long-term aspirations, from our focus on what matters—our relationships with God and with one another.

The aim of this chapter is to bring a word of encouragement from the Bible and thoughts and ideas thereof that could help the transition period during the pandemic until it is over. Let's begin by looking at the book of Joshua and the transition after the death of Moses to the leadership of Joshua.

> After the death of Moses the Lord's servant, the Lord spoke to Joshua son of Nun, Moses' assistant. He said, "Moses my servant is dead. Therefore, the time has come for you to lead these people, the Israelites, across the Jordan River into the land I am giving them. I promise you what I promised Moses: 'Wherever you set foot, you will be on land I have given you—from the Negev wilderness in the south to the Lebanon mountains in the north, from the Euphrates River in the east to the Mediterranean Sea in the west, including all the land of the Hittites.' No one will be able to stand against you as long as you live. For I will be with you as I was with Moses. I will not fail you or abandon you. "Be strong and courageous, for you are the one who will lead these people to possess all the land I swore to their

> ancestors I would give them. Be strong and very courageous. Be careful to obey all the instructions Moses gave you. Do not deviate from them, turning either to the right or to the left. Then you will be successful in everything you do. Study this Book of Instruction continually. Meditate on it day and night so you will be sure to obey everything written in it. Only then will you prosper and succeed in all you do. This is my command—be strong and courageous! Do not be afraid or discouraged. For the Lord your God is with you wherever you go." (Joshua 1:1-9)

Let's look at various aspects of this passage and draw out lessons that we can apply to our current situation.

JOSHUA: MOSES' SERVANT

Joshua, who only came to the scene when the children of Israel went to war against Amalekites (see Exodus 17:9), was a *sharat*, an aide or helper to Moses and served as a close confidant. The death of Moses and the prospects of being the leader of at least one million people during their journey probably gave Joshua sleepless nights and cold chills. Joshua had depended on Moses to hear from God and talk to the people. With Moses gone, he was the one on the hot seat, so to speak.

His closeness to Moses would also mean he was mourning Moses's death. Joshua relied on Moses in all situations for leadership, spiritual direction, and anything else needed at the moment. After Moses passed away, the people were probably comparing him with Moses who we are told talked to God as a man would talk to another man (see Exodus 33:11). It's reasonable to suppose that Joshua must have felt devastated and inadequate like many have felt during the COVID-19 pandemic. It was to this Joshua that God spoke. It was Joshua who heard the voice of the Lord.

I have observed that God talks to His people when they are in a valley or low place in their lives. For example, the voice of the Lord came to Jeremiah whilst he was in prison (Jeremiah 33:1). In the story, Jeremiah, called to be a prophet to the nations (Jeremiah 1:5), was shut up in prison but God spoke to him there—in the low place. Another example is Jacob when he was going to meet his brother after he left Laban's household. The last time they had been together was when Jacob had cheated his brother and obtained his birthright and their father's blessing. Twenty years later, he was going to be reconnected with his brother.

Jacob was so scared about the prospects of meeting his brother that he divided his family and livestock out of fear that his brother would take revenge and attack them (he hoped that if one group was attacked, the other would escape). He also sent emissaries to meet his brother before they came into contact with one another. It was at this point of fear—his low point—that Jacob met and wrestled with the Lord and the Lord blessed him (Genesis 32). Both Jeremiah and Jacob heard from the Lord when they were at a low point—in a valley. If you were or are in a valley because of the pandemic or some other situation, know that you are in a perfect position for God to speak to you like he did to those two men.

Let's look at one more example from the life of Isaiah. We are told that the word of the Lord came to Isaiah the year King Uzziah died (see Isaiah 6:1). To understand Isaiah's context, you should know that Uzziah came to power when he was only 16 years and reigned for 52 years, finally dying from leprosy. Tradition also has it that Isaiah's father Amoz (a prominent man) was a brother to king Amaziah, father to Uzziah, and so Uzziah and Isaiah were first cousins.

Therefore, Isaiah was in the house of God, perhaps asking a lot of questions when he had an encounter with God. Isaiah's situation reminds me of the times in Kenya when our first president, Jomo Kenyatta, died in 1978 after fifteen years of rule and then President Daniel Arap Moi's death in 2002 after 24 years in power. In both instances, people cried. They felt devastated after their leader's demise. Isaiah had similar sadness and pain and was in the house of God, but while asking his questions, he saw God and God spoke to Him. God speaks to us in our lowest times so the pandemic and ensuing season of hardship have been a time to hear from the Lord. I hope that's true for you and that you will remember this truth when your next valley experience comes.

END OF AN ERA

Let's return to the story of Moses and Joshua. The death of God's servant Moses was an end of an era when Joshua found himself without his master and mentor. Let's examine that to see how we can apply the lessons to our current situation. By reminding Joshua about Moses' death, God was telling Joshua he was entering a time of change in which he would see God's faithfulness in a new way. That is true in the post COVID-19 period.

What's more, like the death of Moses, the time of change for us has come rapidly even though Joshua had some warning but we did not. Nevertheless, the lesson is that we must anticipate change and actually plan for it as best we can, even though we cannot actually know the exact nature of the change.

In Luke 24, we are told of an incident involving Mary Magdalene, Joanna, Mary the mother of James, and several other women. These women got to the tomb where Jesus' body had been laid but there was nobody there. Instead, two men appeared to them wearing dazzling robes. The women were terrified after having been distressed not to find the body of the Lord. They were helpless and hopeless, only then to face those two strangers. Then the angels asked what seemed like a bizarre question to them: "Why are you looking among the dead for someone who is alive?" (Luke 24:6-7).

The angels reminded them that Jesus had predicted He would rise from the dead and then, of course, the women saw Jesus and realized He was alive as promised. Their lives would never be the same. Things had changed forever in ways they were yet to discover. The same is true for us who endured the pandemic. Church life, work, and relationships will all be different if in no other way than we will have greater appreciation for what we have because we endured a season when we had not.

Like Joshua and the disciples after the resurrection, the current situation is ushering in a time when God will show

His faithfulness to us in a new way. When Moses died, the "good old days" were done and gone. That's important to remember because our past can distract us from moving forward as we fight to maintain what is no more. It was similar to when we were moving to Australia.

The old days of living in Kenya were over and it was time for us to move on, but we tried to hold on to our way of life we had enjoyed in Kenya. We thought we knew what to expect, but Australia was an entirely new experience in which we had to trust the Lord for a new destiny that we had not previously considered. Even now when people have lost loved ones and others have suffered economic loss through the pandemic, God is still on the throne and there is now a new day.

THE ASSURANCE

In the story of Moses and Joshua, we see God's unwavering promise go from one generation to another:

> "I promise you what I promised Moses: 'Wherever you set foot, you will be on land I have given you—from the Negev wilderness in the south to the Lebanon mountains in the north, from the Euphrates River in the east to the Mediterranean Sea in the west, including all the land of the Hittites'" (Joshua 1:3-4).

In the context, God assured Joshua that despite the passing of Moses, the promises He had made to Abraham (see Genesis 15:18) and had reiterated to Moses in Deuteronomy 1:7 remained. Nothing had changed even though the leadership had transitioned. The same is true for 2021 and beyond. God's promises remain intact.

However, God also reminded Joshua that it was time for him to lead the Israelites across the Jordan River into the land of promise. In other words, this was not the time to lose focus on inheriting the promise, which was possession of the land. Even though Joshua was probably at a low point in the aftermath of Moses' passing, he still had to lead.

The same is true for God's leaders during and after COVID. This is a time to lead, not to try and preserve or recapture the past, and to take people into their and our promised land. Throughout this season, I have reflected on Philippians 3:13-16:

> No, dear brothers and sisters, I have not achieved it, but I focus on this one thing: Forgetting the past and looking forward to what lies ahead, I press on to reach the end of the race and receive the heavenly prize for which God, through Christ Jesus, is calling us. Let all who are spiritually mature agree on these things. If you disagree on some point, I believe God will make it plain to you. But we must hold on to the progress we have already made.

Paul reminded us that we must hold on to the progress we have already made and press on to the mark of the high calling we have in Christ. God did not allow Joshua to stay where he and the people were; they had to move to apprehend the promises of God. Each of us must do the same.

"AS I WAS WITH MOSES, I WILL BE WITH YOU."

COVID-19 has produced great concern among people for their safety and that of their loved ones. This is another lesson we can take from the story of Joshua, for while God expected the people to move on, He promised His protection as they did. In fact, it seems that God is always telling His people to move on, relying on the promise that He goes with them to watch over them. Perhaps Joshua had feelings of inadequacy as he faced leading in the place of Moses who talked to God "face to face."

God's love is never-ending and goes from generation to generation. As Paul pointed out, God's love and faithfulness are demonstrated in times of difficulties and trials and in our weakness (see 2 Corinthians 12:9). When we are most vulnerable, that is the time for God's strength to be revealed. Moses' leadership depended on God being with him, not necessarily his great leadership skills—though he was a great leader.

In the time of COVID and after, God assures us that as He was with the people in the wilderness and with His disciples in the early church, He is and will be with us. He neither leaves not forsakes His people (see Deuteronomy 31:6; Hebrews 13:5). Maybe you are scared of what lies ahead,

God's word to you is that His presence goes with you into the future. He saw COVID, He led you through it, and He will continue to lead you on the other side.

"NO ONE WILL BE ABLE TO STAND AGAINST YOU."

In times of crisis, there always seem to be messengers of doom and impending harm. Not only does God say He will be with you but also assures you of His defense and protection. Yes, there will be enemies, even invisible ones, that will oppose and block you. The journey to your destiny and the possession of the promises of God is never an easy one. God does not promise His people a situation where they're not going to be opposed.

As a matter fact, He promises his people they will overcome their enemies with no one able to stand against them. That means they will come against you but they're not going to be able to withstand you. How will you ever know the truth of this promise if you have no opponents to overcome? These enemies come to show you the power and presence of God.

Are you in a situation you cannot control? Our help is in God, as we have been reminded during the pandemic. It was encouraging to hear leaders, even leaders of government, echo this sentiment. Australia's Scot Morrison said, "I'm in prayer. My prayer knees are getting a good workout" (Morrison, S., PM of Australia, 2020). President Uhuru Kenyatta of Kenya declared, "Even Science needs prayers" (Kenyatta U., President, Kenya, 2020). Andrew Holiness, prime minister of Jamaica, led his nation in prayer and said, "Let us pray. God is for us, and will not abandon us at this time of need."

"BE STRONG AND COURAGEOUS."

Another difference between the ministry of Moses and Joshua was one of intent. Moses' ministry focused more on liberation whereas Joshua's focus was more on war and conquest. This was going to demand courage and strength, hence the exhortation for Joshua to be strong and courageous—a command rather than a request. He had to get used to times of warfare and battle and the same message has been true during and will remain true after the pandemic.

We all have had to be encouraged to continue exercising our faith trust and hope. Joshua had to manifest strength of character and resolve. He could not look at the circumstances but had to focus on the Lord. COVID signifies a pivotal time in the age of the Church where the Church may be set on a course of confrontation with forces that are opposed to its very existence. This will certainly require every believer to have courage and strength like Joshua.

However, we can be encouraged of God's presence in the battle, knowing the battle is not ours but the Lord's as the Scriptures declare (see 2 Chronicles 20:20). A Christian's battles are not fought using human strength or applying human weaponry and ingenuity but are won through reliance on God's help and strength.

In Joshua's situation, God had already provided the way for them by giving the Israelites His word in the form of the law of Moses. Joshua was told to depend on His word and instructions, to meditate on it day and night, for his success and prosperity depended on it. Faith depends on hearing and hearing the word of the Lord. His instructions were to study the word of the Lord and meditate on it.

CONCLUSION

What is the message to the Church in this season? This is the time to stay focused on God and His Kingdom, understanding what matters to God at this time. The current crisis, like the time of the death of Moses, is a time to reassure His people that He is still their God, like He was before the pandemic. His plan for eternity is not derailed. He is coming back, and so the Church should not be distracted from focusing on the Kingdom. We are indeed a people who may be distressed but we are not to be distracted!

2

POWER OF PRAYER

This chapter is a prophetic message from the Lord on how we should respond generally in difficult times but particularly in this time of the pandemic. It is a message about the now. We are passing through a difficult season, It's a different time. In such a time we have had adjust and do what is right as we cooperated with many things such as social distancing, self-isolating or being vaccinated, which is now mandatory in many places.

But when all is said and done, we have to look to God. We should not be afraid of anything, because our God is in control. He is on the throne. I was talking to a dear friend and he reminded me of the fact that during this pandemic, the Lord is still on the throne. We would and should be scared if He wasn't. The song says that there is no shadow of turning in Him, come rain or sunshine. Even though the world is upside down, the Lord is still on the throne. Because He is there, I can face tomorrow.

Paul said that in Him we live and move and have our being. We are confident in Him. We are grateful that we belong to God and know God. We know also, at the same time, that we should be interceding, listening for something. I hear in my heart things about coronavirus. We have seen that the mighty power, the United States of America, is experiencing a very difficult time. For the first time Americans are actually badly divided along political lines.

In Australia, at one time we were talking about our territory covered by bushfires as never seen before. Economically, we hear that the Australian dollar and interest rates are at levels that have not been seen in many years. So, whether we are talking about economics, nature, or politics, the theme is that of rapid and adverse changes. We are in a situation where we have one thing, then it is suddenly overtaken by another.

Then we came to the period of the COVID-19 pandemic and all of a sudden, the affairs of the entire world changed. The governments and their systems have been tried, the supply chain and other systems have been tested. The health systems have been stretched as never before. Scenes of crazy shoppers at the onset of the pandemic all over the world were watched in disbelief. Thank God that today we can watch media clips on social media of what is happening almost minute by minute all over the world.

It's interesting that in America in the early days of the pandemic, coupled with the politics of the day, people queued to buy guns early the morning in anticipation of civil unrest. Supermarkets were sites of crazy shopping. Interesting too the way that fear drove wisdom out the window. For example, there was news of people unexplainably stockpiling crates of fresh produce and lots of rolls of toilet paper!

TURNING TO GOD IN PRAYER

In the early days of the pandemic, there were several pictures of people praying. Three clips in particular got my attention. One was in a hallway of a hospital with medical workers in scrubs and operating room protective gear with hands raised to heaven and in prayer. There was another of people kneeling down in Brazil singing *Porque Ele Vive*, a Portuguese version of *Because he lives I can face tomorrow* by Fernandinho. Yet another was one in which mechanics and motorcycle operators popularly known in Kenya as *Boda Boda* operators in Ruaka near Nairobi laid down their tools of trade to kneel in the middle of the street and pray for their nation. These stood out to me because in all three there was a realization of the helplessness and vulnerability of humanity and the need to turn to God in prayer.

These events were significant for two reasons. First was the fact that the medics, despite their knowledge of medical science, realized that COVID-19 was bigger than medical science alone could handle. The second thing I thought as I watched these people praying was that they knew there is a God above COVID-19 who is able to do exceedingly, abundantly above all that anyone can ask, think, or imagine. Third is the realization that we can turn to God because He answers prayers, He asks us to pray at all times (see 1 Thessalonians 5:18), to call to Him when we are in trouble (see Jeremiah 33:1), and to keep praying (see Matthew 7:7), doing so persistently (see Luke 18:1). May I encourage us that the power of prayer is the power of God.

When turning to God in prayer, we are saying that we can trust the God who will heal our land as stated in 2 Chronicles 7:14. A few verses before that verse, Solomon commenced a dialogue with God. God told him that He has heard his prayer: "Then one night the Lord appeared to Solomon saying, "I have heard your prayer and have chosen this Temple as the place for making sacrifices. At times I might shut up the heavens so that no rain falls, or command grasshoppers to devour your crops, or send plagues among you." (2 Chronicles 7:12-13, my paraphrase).

God said to Solomon, "I have heard your prayer." That reminds me of the story in Genesis concerning Hagar. In Genesis 16, Hagar was running away from Sarah when an angel of the Lord came to her and told her that God had heard her cry, saying, "You're pregnant with child and that child shall be called Ishmael because the Lord hears." The Lord hears. I like the words Hagar uttered in that context, *Beer-lahai-roi,* which means "well of the Living One who sees me." God is one who sees from Heaven what is happening on planet Earth. He encourages us to call unto Him and He will answer. He reminds us in this season of COVID-19 that He will answer when we call on His name.

PRAYER IS FAITH IN PRACTICE

To help us understand the power of prayer, we read the exhortation given by the Apostle James:

> Are any of you suffering hardships? You should pray. Are any of you happy? You should sing praises. Are any of you sick? You should call for the elders of the church to come and pray over you, anointing you with oil in the name of the Lord. Such a prayer offered in faith will heal the sick, and the Lord will make you well. And if you have committed any sins, you will be forgiven. Confess your sins to each other and pray for each other so that you may be healed. The earnest prayer of a righteous person has great power and produces wonderful results. Elijah was as human as we are, and yet when he prayed earnestly that no rain would fall, none fell for three and a half years! Then, when he prayed again, the sky sent down rain and the earth began to yield its crops (James 5:13-18).

To understand the encouragement, it is important to remember that the epistle of James was written to Jewish believers scattered abroad because they faced persecution and difficult times. James talked about practical faith as opposed to a faith that is only based on dogma. James covered practical topics such as endurance in trials, listening to the word and doing what its says, the pure religion of doing acts of charity, not despising and looking down upon the poor. All this is a practical faith that is expressed through works, rather than through mere following of laws.

James concluded the epistle by emphasizing the power of prayer. Like the responses I witnessed from Brazil, Kenya, and America, James was reminding his readers that they have to look to God in prayer. It is from here that we learn four key lessons he reveals about prayer: the power of prayer, the need to call elders to pray, the nature of prayer, and the nature of the people who should pray.

1. POWER OF PRAYER

The first point in James' letter is the emphasis on the power of prayer. In this epistle about practical faith, we are told that the practical faith activity in situations is our faith response in prayer. One of the most encouraging thing I saw during the pandemic was to see national leaders encourage their people to pray. Speaking to Kenyans on the National Prayer Day on 21 March, 2020, President Uhuru Kenyatta stated, "Even science needs God." That was profound!

In similar manner, the Australian prime minister, Scott Morrison, joined the Australian Christian Churches (ACC) and organized prayers online from his parliamentary office, urging people to pray for the prime ministers and presidents so they could make good decisions during the pandemic. These and other national leaders realized that there is a God in Heaven who responds to prayer and who is above any power—economic, political, or otherwise. The way that we exercise our faith practically is by praying to God, for prayer works. Even when systems are tried or they fail, we can turn to God in prayer because God never fails.

2. CALL ELDERS

The second point on prayer in James's exhortation is found in verse 14 where he encouraged the believers to call elders of the church for prayers and verse 16 which encourages prayers one for another and confession of sins one to another. James's encouragement assumes Christians were living in fellowship with one another as a body of believers (see Acts 2:42), what we would refer to in the Greek language as *koinonia*. Koinonia mean "intimate spiritual communion and participative sharing in a common religious commitment and spiritual community," speaking of deep intimate fellowship with the Lord and with one another. A key element of *koinonia* is living and agreeing together, confessing and forgiving the sins of one another, harmony and togetherness of believers, best captured by yet another Greek word for agreement, *sumpheneo.*

This word is the one from which we derive the word symphony as in an orchestra. In a symphony orchestra, there has to be harmony, meaning that every member of the orchestra has to read from the same script. This is the teaching taught by Jesus in Matthew 18:15-20. Included in *koinonia* is the aspect of church, *ecclesi*a in Greek, with legitimate authority vested in church elders or *presbuteros* in Greek, similar in Hebrew to members of the council of elders referred to as the *Sanhedrin.*

What's my point? James emphasized the fact that the prayer of faith recognizes the authority of spiritual leaders and the honour bestowed upon them. Agreement in prayer and living in community are vital to the body of believers functioning together and also necessary for the prayers of the saints to be answered as was the case in early church. Harmony and love are vital for the manifestation of the power of God as He answers prayer, so much so that Christ prayed for the unity of the body of Christ (see John 17:20-21).

Oneness of mind and purpose in the body, primarily in the local assembly and the nation, are vital prerequisites to prayers being answered. Effective prayer is assigned to the Church as patterned by God's design of fellowship in the body of Christ. Could God be calling us to back to prayers as a church in the pandemic season and its aftermath?

3. NATURE OF PRAYER

The third point that emerges from the letter is the nature and type of prayer. There are many aspects to effective prayer. First is what we have already covered, the oneness, unity, and authority of the local church. Second, prayer is offered in faith—faith in God's promises. Third, prayer is described as earnest prayer—effectual fervent prayer as stated in the King James version (KJV) of the Bible. This powerful prayer is described by the word *energeo* in Greek, which means *to be operative, be at work, put forth power, be mighty in, shew forth self, work, accomplish something.*

This describes offering focused, passion-filled petitions to God, such as those prayed by Hannah, Daniel, David, and Jesus (John 17). Such prayers have great power and produce wonderful results that can even heal the sick. One prayer that has been quoted greatly in this pandemic period is Psalm 91:

> This I declare about the Lord: He alone is my refuge, my place of safety; he is my God, and I trust him. For he will rescue you from every trap and protect you from deadly disease. He will cover you with his feathers. He will shelter you with his wings. His faithful promises are your armor and protection. Do not be afraid of the terrors of the night, nor the arrow that flies in the day. Do not dread the disease that stalks in darkness, nor the disaster that strikes at midday. Though a thousand fall at your side, though ten thousand are dying around you, these evils will not touch you. (Psalm 91:2-7).

4. MAN OF LIKE PASSIONS

The fourth point addresses who should pray, which James described as men of "like passions,"ordinary men or women in this case, not extraordinary or elite people. In James 5:17, we are told that Elijah was a man subject to passions like us. In other words, Elijah was pretty much human as we are. He was no angel or superior celestial being. In James 5:16, James exhorted us with the words "effectual fervent prayer of a righteous man" which "availeth much." In other words, prayer is effective and produces great results.

However, the phrase "righteous man" talks about a right standing with God, a position of moral uprightness and character. This addresses the need to pray from the designate position of right standing with God through Christ as children of God. We will see the effect of our prayer because of our right standing with God. Who should pray? The person who prays powerful prayers is here characterized as a righteous ordinary person, all that is required of a man or woman who prays. This is the person who fits well in the *koinonia*.

Prophetically, I see we are entering a time in which the power of God is going to be manifested as never before in modern times through ordinary believers, people of right standing with God—not mighty men or women who are superheroes. Instead, they are God's righteous children made so through the powerful work of the cross, the cleansing power of the blood of Jesus our Lord and Saviour.

CONCLUSION

In this chapter, we have looked at power in prayer and the fact that God is calling His church, His government on earth, His *ecclesia,* to prayer. As we are told in Haggai 2 and again in Hebrews, we live in the time when God is shaking every system—government, social, economic, and even religious. But as promised, the Church of Jesus Christ will not be shaken, but instead it will make manifest the wisdom of God to any powers who oppose it. The Church will prevail through prayer by faith, for the power of prayer is the power of God.

This prayer is aligned with God's pattern of building of the body of Christ in *koinonia*, the fellowship of God's people. These are ordinary people not superheroes, whose only qualification is their right standing with God through Christ, God is planning for the display of His glory on earth. In the next chapter, we will talk more about prayer as a vital practice in the time we are living in.

3

PRAY WITHOUT CEASING

In the previous chapter, we talked about the power of prayer. In this chapter, let's look at not only the power of prayer, but also the principle that prayer ought to be persistent. Jesus taught His disciples that they should pray without ceasing, never giving up. Let's look at Luke 18 that shows us the story when Jesus imparted this truth:

> One day Jesus told his disciples a story to show that they should always pray and never give up. "There was a judge in a certain city," he said, "who neither feared God nor cared about people. A widow of that city came to him repeatedly, saying, 'Give me justice in this dispute with my enemy.' The judge ignored her for a while, but finally he said to himself, 'I don't fear God or care about people, but this woman is driving me crazy. I'm going to see that she

> gets justice, because she is wearing me out with her constant requests!'"
>
> Then the Lord said, "Learn a lesson from this unjust judge. Even he rendered a just decision in the end. So don't you think God will surely give justice to his chosen people who cry out to him day and night? Will he keep putting them off? I tell you, he will grant justice to them quickly! But when the Son of Man returns, how many will he find on the earth who have faith?" (Luke 18: 1-8).

Jesus and His disciples were between Galilee and Jerusalem and that's important to know because this is when Jesus began teaching His followers about the Kingdom. At that point in time, He discussed a number of things regarding the Kingdom, and then He addressed the subject of faith for His Kingdom citizens. It seems that not giving up in prayer is an important practice in God's Kingdom.

GOD'S PRIORITY

It's important to understand that the Kingdom is God's priority. In Genesis, we read that God directed Adam and Eve to fill the earth and have dominion over it, which was also an expression of God's Kingdom. He would rule as King and they would be His subjects, carrying out His will in accord with their own purpose and gifts.

Then we know that Satan came and usurped control. The best way to think about what happened is to compare it to colonization. The god of this world came and invaded the world of Adam and Eve. Of course we know that their world was God's world for the earth belongs to the Lord. However, the usurper came and the kingdom of darkness set up a rival kingdom. We learn that things got so bad by the time of Noah that God destroyed everyone except Noah and his family because God intended to re-establish His Kingdom.

In the book of Genesis, we read that God was looking for a person He could use like He had Adam and found him—a man by the name of Abraham. God's desire was to make Abraham a nation through his kindred through which to establish His kingdom. We see in Genesis 28 that the promise and command given to Adam was applied to Israel, that they were to be fruitful and multiply. That happened, but when we read Ezekiel 34, we see just like in the time of Noah, all was not well. Israel, the nation God has established for Himself, was having problems. The rulers and leaders of the kingdom had failed Him.

Then God embarked on a double mission. He had to redeem or save His people Israel but also reach the sheep outside those sheep pens, namely the Gentiles. That is why He sent His own son Jesus Christ to redeem and restore the Kingdom back to Himself once having wrested it away from the colonizer. From that, He was then to establish the Church. God wants His Kingdom to be proclaimed and realized through the Church.

This has been God's work through the ages. It's important to understand God's idea of the Kingdom because Jesus came preaching the Kingdom. His Kingdom purpose was paramount above every other thing. It's God's preoccupation. God's purpose on earth is really about His Kingdom. When Jesus came to earth, His message was clear. He said to repent for the Kingdom of heaven was nigh.

In Matthew 6:33, Jesus said we are not to look for raiment or clothing or food as the children of this world frantically seek these things. He said, "Seek ye first the kingdom of God and his righteousness and all these things will be added unto you" (Matthew 6:33). The tragedy for many in the church today is that their lives have become about those things. It has become about prosperity. Jesus said to seek first the Kingdom of God and these other things would be added because the Kingdom was more important—to be the highest priority in a believer's life.

Something was to be more significant for us than just raiment, food, or the car we drive. It was about God's Kingdom and His purpose. God is cleaning up the Church so we can focus back on the Kingdom. Jesus said in Luke 17:20-21 that the Kingdom is within you. We should pay attention to the context of what He is saying when He then moves on to tell the parable of the woman and the unjust judge in Luke 18. His whole message was about the Kingdom.

FAITH AND PRAYER

Jesus was a master teacher who in Luke 18 was teaching about faith, asking if He would find faith when He returned. The focus of this faith was in the context of prayer. That is why He asked that, if when the Son of Man comes he would he find people who believe (see Luke 18:8). The main way faith is exercised on earth is through prayer which is the means by which Kingdom reality is achieved—or not. Whether it's Lazarus rising from the dead or Elijah calling down the fire or rain, it's all done through prayer.

Kingdom realities are realized on earth through prayer. That's why it is paramount that we know and exercise the power in prayer. Whether we are talking about Black Lives Matter, or poverty in Africa, or other injustices of this world (even the pandemic), God's Kingdom purposes will be realized through prayer. I can't overemphasize this.

God is calling us back to prayer. The Bible says, "When my people who are called by my name shall humble themselves and pray, and turn from their wicked ways, then I will hear from heaven" (2 Chronicles 7:14). Why was there a temple in Jerusalem? So that people could come before God in prayer in times of peace and war. Why was there a synagogue? Why was there a tabernacle? It was that the people would come to the Lord in prayer.

Let me break it down again. The Kingdom of God and the knowledge of the Kingdom are what He was teaching about in Luke 18. And the expression of the Kingdom was praying in faith. How is faith activated? It is exercised by and through prayer. The principle He was teaching is important to understand and it was that we should always pray and not give up.

In this time of the pandemic, more than ever we ought to be praying without giving up, even when we don't see results. Sometimes if we don't see results over time, we can become discouraged. The children of Israel remained in captivity in Babylon for 70 years. He told them they should pray and seek His face and when they did, He promised to restore their fortunes. He has plans, and we will access those plans through prayer. It may take a while. He may tarry for a moment, but eventually He will act and it will come to pass.

Mark wrote in Mark 1:35 that before anybody awakened, Jesus was up in prayer. Then look at the context of Luke 12:32: "Don't fear little flock for it is your father's good pleasure to give you the Kingdom." It's the Father's good pleasure to give us the Kingdom and it is what we should be seeking. Let's now look at the entire story of the woman and the unjust judge in Luke 18:

> One day Jesus told his disciples a story to show that they should always pray and never give up. "There was a judge in a certain city," he said, "who neither feared God nor cared about people. A widow of that city came to him repeatedly, saying, 'Give me justice in this dispute with my enemy.' The judge ignored her for a while, but finally he said to himself, 'I don't fear God or care about people, but this woman is driving me crazy. I'm going to see that she gets justice, because she is wearing me out with her constant requests'" (Luke 18:1-6).

It's important to make it a point here that the woman in Luke 18 represents the elect who pray day and night. Let's look at the unjust judge, the widow, and last of all, God's vindication of the elect as important lessons to learn.

In verse four, we see that the judge ignored the widow for a while. The unjust judge represents the enemy or enemies of God. Referring to John 10, Jesus said the thief comes to steal, kill, and destroy. The shepherd comes through the door or the gate. Another way the thief can come in is to jump over the wall. Jesus described the good shepherd as the one who comes in through and then defends the gate, keeping it open and safe for others. He sleeps at the door, doing so to protect the sheep. All these things really tie Jesus in as the Shepherd. The people understood. They understood the Old Testament prophecies. They understood the Law.

The unjust judge represents the oppressive forces and enemies of God's people. The enemy is the injustice of this world and the oppressive forces of darkness in God's creation that are at work because of the Fall. God's purpose is to redeem His creation, including man. God is always looking out redemptively to His own, those who stray away from Him. He wants to demonstrate His Kingdom power.

The Bible says in 2 Chronicles 9:16 that the eyes of the Lord search the whole earth to strengthen those whose hearts are fully committed to Him. At this time, He's looking to strengthen those who have suffered injustice. When man looks to God, God redeems man and brings him into His redemptive purposes. The story of the unjust judge points out that there will be justice but it will be eventually corrected by the power of God.

HEARTBREAK

During the pandemic, my heart broke for America when I saw militia with rifles in the streets. If you're an American reader, I want you to know I was and still am praying for you. America has been a blessed nation and has blessed many others. A lot of people dream of going to America. We have learned to call it the land of opportunity. Now we see things in America that we could not imagine would ever happen: militia, rifles in the streets, mobs, and looting.

God revealed to me that Africa received independence from colonization through shedding of blood and through a revolution. I don't believe that is God's ideal way. God delivered the children of Israel many times without anyone shooting an arrow. I believe in the power of God and He wants to show His power against injustice.

There's a spiritual result that cannot be achieved by protests in the streets. We're dealing with situations only the God of heaven can deal with in a just manner. The unjust systems and rulers of this world are not about to be overcome by a simple protest. God's plan is His salvation that goes beyond just forgiveness of sin. It is beyond deliverance. It is rescue and deliverance from all manner of injustice and evil. That is what the story of the unjust judge represents.

The second thing we should look at in the story is the widow. We read in verse three that a widow of that city came to the judge repeatedly saying, "Give me justice in this dispute with my enemy." The woman represented the elect of God. You are the children of the Kingdom, the elect of God, the children of the Kingdom, and God will grant you justice by granting you the Kingdom. I'm reminded of Ephesians 1:3-4:

> All praise to God, the father of our Lord Jesus Christ, who has blessed us with every spiritual blessing in the heavenly realms, because we are united with Christ. Even before he made the world, God loved us and chose us in Christ to be Holy and without fault in his eyes.

Remember, this was written to the *Gentile* believers in Ephesus. Even before He made the world, God loved us and chose us in Christ to be holy and without fault—even the Gentiles. That is His Kingdom purpose. We know the widow in the story represents the elect of God and His Kingdom purposes to be fulfilled through them.

Let me mention something about the elect. They will receive the justice of God. That is God's purpose. That is why we repent. Through repentance the elect receive salvation because they have turned to God. They come to Jesus Christ and receive salvation and they will ultimately receive justice. In fact, here are five things I see concerning the elect in this story:

1. They will receive justice as I have already written.
2. They will be drawn to God and taught of God as Jesus said in John 6:43-44. Jesus informed His disciples that there were others outside Israel who had to come into the Kingdom. They would be one flock, but made up of black, white, yellow, Jewish, and non-Jewish people. That flock is the elect, the church of Jesus Christ. He's coming for a Church without wrinkle or spot—the elect. That's what God is preparing us for in these end times. Christ said He would build His church and the gates of hell would not prevail against it.
3. The elect are called in by His name. In John

10:16, we read, "My sheep hear my voice and I call them by name." We read in Isaiah 45:4, "My people, I know them by name." God calls the elect by name because He knows them by name.

4. They shall not be deceived. In Matthew 24:24, we are told, "For the sake of the elect the time will be shortened." The enemy wants to deceive even the elect if he can, but they shall not be deceived.
5. As we saw in Matthew chapter 24:24, "the day of suffering for the just will be shortened." When there's suffering in these last days, the days of suffering will be shortened for the sake of the elect.

THE WIDOW

Let's stay focused on the widow a little longer and see what else she teaches us about the elect of God.

1. She knew her Kingdom rights. She was persistent. She positioned herself to receive the benefits of those rights. Jesus described it as His sheep knowing His voice. He knows them and when they call, He will answer. They know who they are and they know their God according to Daniel 11:32: "They that know their God, they will be strong and do exploits." The elect know their God and their Kingdom rights. They call on God through prayer. Jesus is wondering whether there will be many elect who will take full advantage of their rights. Will He find faith? Will He find people trusting God when he returns?
2. The widow didn't give up. She waited long and didn't think, "I tried last time. It didn't work. I've called on Him. He didn't care." The widow didn't care what kind of man the judge was. Even though he had a reputation for being unjust, she kept on going and asking. The elect

don't care how many people have tried or what has happened in the past. They keep on pressing and calling on God.

3. The judge ignored her for a while, but finally he said, "I don't fear God or care about people, but this woman is driving me crazy. I'm going to see that she gets justice, because she's wearing me out with her constant requests." That is the voice of the enemy. What we see here is that the enemy will become worn out. The Bible tells us, "Resist the devil and he will flee" (see James 4:7). Persistence wears away devilish resistance. God will vindicate his own speedily with a breakthrough. Jesus was telling them that God will deliver them, even if He tarries. God was teaching them tenacity and persistence in prayer.

Hebrews 10:35-39 says,

> So do not throw away this confident trust in the Lord. Remember the great reward it brings you! Patient endurance is what you need now, so that you will continue to do God's will. Then you will receive all that he has promised." The trial of faith produces endurance and character. As we wait and call on the Lord, he develops our character. Maturity is developing and that means God is developing a mature church. There are no diapers in heaven. Heaven is for nuanced, mature believers who offer Him praise and worship in spirit and in truth.

We've talked about the woman and the judge and what they represent. The last thing I want to talk about is God and His character: "Don't you think God will surely give justice to his chosen people who cry out to him both day and night. Or will he keep putting them off? I tell you; he will grant justice to them quickly." Unlike the unjust judge, by comparison we learn that God cares and will grant justice not because He is worn out from our asking but because He is exhilarated by it. Also notable is the phrase used for God's action. He will act promptly, with speed, indicating a sense of decisiveness and timeliness when He moves to act.

ELIJAH

Recently God reminded me of the story in Elijah's life when there was no rain but then he prayed and it rained as told in James 5:17-18. Later in the New Testament, James wrote that Elijah was a man of like passions as ours. Seven times he sent his servant to go and check outside to see if rain clouds were forming. He persisted and finally, his prayer was answered and it rained.

Elijah is as an example for us of a man who prayed, and only eventually something happened. James told us he didn't give up and Jesus taught that we ought to pray with the same perseverance, to pray without ceasing. Pray in all circumstances. Pray about everything. Our response to injustice needs to be prayer because Kingdom purposes are realized only through prayer.

We are at a point where we do not embrace prayer. Our prayer meetings are not well attended even though the power is in prayer. God is taking us back to the point where we can go to Him in prayer as a first response, not as a last one.

Jesus taught his disciples about prayer but today, we focus on a lot of other things. We teach classes and there is nothing wrong with that. Jesus' model, however, was to stop what He was doing, teach the people or His disciples, and then pray—sometimes all night. He modeled a life of prayer. God is calling us back to prayer so we can know and experience the power of prayer.

God is speaking to us in this time of shaking, but let's look up because God is coming. He's going to come in power and in glory. In other words, the Lord will vindicate His elect after all is said and done. In the pandemic and its aftermath, God wants people who will pray without ceasing. He wants people who will pray regardless of what rules or lockdowns or other inconveniences are established and no matter what injustices we see or encounter.

It's interesting how the poor and rich nations of the world were reduced to the same level during the pandemic.

Everything has been reduced because everything has been shaken. That is why we need to pray with confidence and without ceasing.

4

WE ARE MOVING FORWARD

In 2020, the world experienced a shaking like never before seen in other chapters of history—and it's still not over as I write. There's been a complete shift and shaking of every area. I read some beautiful summaries online during this time. Here are some of them:

- We fell asleep in one world and woke up in another.
- Suddenly Disney is out of magic.
- The Chinese world is no longer a fortress.
- Hugs and kisses suddenly became weapons.
- Not visiting parents and friends becomes an act of love.

- Suddenly you realize that power, beauty, and money can't get you the oxygen you're fighting for.
- The world continues its life, and it's beautiful. It only puts humans in cages. I think it's sending us a message. You're not necessary. The air, the earth, the water, and sky without you are fine. When you come back, remember you are my guest, not my Masters (Anonymous).

I'm not saying that I'm agreeing with every one of those statements, but they certainly brought the message home that things have changed.

There is another one. the prime minister of Australia, Scott Morrison, said, "The new normal has become your normal." In a few short months, God took away everything we worshiped. I'm not saying God caused the pandemic, but I'm saying God has used it to strip away almost everything in life and culture that we have taken for granted for a long time.

In a sense, He has said, "You want to worship in big groups, I will shut down the stadium and arenas. Do you want to worship musicians? I will shut down every venue. You want to worship actors? I will shut down theaters. You want to worship money? I will shut down the economy and the stock markets. You want to worship your bodies? I will close down all the gyms. You want to worship your own intellect and pat yourself on the back with graduations? I will close down your schools. You want to place your trust in your friends and not in Me? I'll make sure you can't meet with them physically. You don't want to seek my face and worship me? I will make it where you can't go to church"(Anonymous).

EVERYTHING IS BEING SHAKEN

I don't know who wrote that but it pretty much captures what is happening regarding church and worship. I'm not saying I agree with that, but the bottom line is that there is a shaking. Every time I think about the shaking, I think about the words in the book of Haggai

For this is what the Lord of Heaven's Armies says:

> In just a little while I will again shake the heavens and the earth, the oceans and the dry land. I will shake all the nations, and the treasures of all the nations will be brought to this Temple. I will fill this place with glory, says the LORD of Heaven's Armies" (Haggai 2:6-7).

Hebrews 12 states it a bit differently and involves the church as well as all creation:

> When God spoke from Mount Sinai his voice shook the earth, but now he makes another promise: "Once again I will shake not only the earth but the heavens also. This means that all of creation will be shaken and removed, so that only unshakable things will remain. Since we are receiving a Kingdom that is unshakable, let us be thankful and please God by worshiping him with holy fear and awe" (Hebrews 12:26-28).

What I like about this passage is it talks about *everything* being shaken. I also thank God that it mentions the fact that we, this is talking about all believers or Christians, have received a Kingdom that is unshakable. We are abiding in Him and continue to worship God with holy fear and awe despite the current shaking.

What is God saying in all this? Again and again, we've heard the verse found in Amos 3:7: "The sovereign Lord never does anything until he reveals his plans to his servants, the prophets." God has not been silent in this season. Even within Scripture itself, we can find a revelation of what God is saying. Peter in his second epistle stated that in the word of God or prophecies are things that have been said that must come to pass. God is never silent because His Word is always speaking.

There are various types of prophecies. One is what I call the catastrophic type, predicting a bad event that is about to come. The second type is basically what God is saying in the midst of the trouble, even in the midst of the pandemic. For example, when the prophet Isaiah came onto the scene and said what was going to happen, it wasn't just so he could predict the future. He spoke to assure the people that what was happening was under God's control and that God was using the circumstances to bring people back to Him. Prophecy should always bring people back, comforting and assuring the people that God is with them. Even when there was (or is) a disaster, He showed how He was going to restore His people.

The prophetic message should give comfort and encouragement that God is with His people during the "now" or coming event, that He is going to be with His people in the future. In short, it should communicate that He cares for His people. At the same time, He is a God of justice, so he would also tell them what would happen and how He would destroy His people if they continued to rebel against Him. My point in writing all that is to say we must position ourselves to hear what God is saying for us in this time that we are in now.

GOD'S PURPOSE

Having said that, let's look at the word of God in Romans 8:28 where it says, "And we know that God causes everything to work together for the good of those who love God and are called according to his purpose for them." This pandemic season was and is working together for good for those who love the Lord and are called according to His purpose. Having read and heard a number of messages, I can say confidently that God wants to demonstrate His power to us.

Paul wrote in Ephesians 3:10, "God's purpose in all this was to use the church to display his wisdom in its rich variety to all the unseen rulers and authorities in the heavenly places." God is calling His own to intimacy with him. He's calling his children to a closer walk with Him. God is preparing His bride and is going to show Himself strong. He yearns for His people to develop an intimate, close walk with Him. He will lead and protect, and provide salvation for His people.

We read in Acts 2:21, "But everyone who calls on the name of the LORD will be saved." The Greek word for salvation is *sozo*, which means *to save, to keep safe, to rescue from danger or destruction, from injury or peril, to save from perishing, from suffering, from disease; to make well, to heal, to preserve, to deliver, to deliver from the penalty of the judgment.* God is going to save

His people and demonstrate His power in the same way that He saved Meshack, Shadrach, and Abednego in Daniel 2. God wants to show Himself as the God of His people, the church of Jesus Christ.

That's why in previous chapters I've shared about the power of prayer and the fact that as the true church of Jesus Christ, we will not be distracted though distressed. In this chapter, I address the concept of the Kingdom which is advancing or moving forward. The Kingdom of God will not stop even if we stop. In the book of Isaiah, the Word says of His Kingdom there shall not be an end.

The Lord Jesus said, "From the day of John the Baptist until now, the Kingdom of heaven has been forcefully advancing and the forceful men lay hold of it" (Matthew 11:12). The Greek word for *advancing* is *biazos* and it has the connotation of a forceful advance. The Kingdom of God is advancing in every situation, including the pandemic. The Church may not be able to meet in big halls or sanctuaries, but the Kingdom of God will not be stopped.

God will always have a remnant of His people, which we will discuss in later chapters. That remnant gets hold of Him and embraces this concept of being forceful. Jesus taught that the Kingdom is advancing through forceful people, which I am referring to as His remnant. Thus this advancement will not involve every follower or believer, excluding those who have fallen by the wayside through lukewarm, carnal living—those who are living as Christians but are double-minded, being drawn back into the world.

However, the remnant are those who know what God's purpose is. They can answer the questions: What's God doing? What's God saying? Where is God taking us? Then they follow God through the answers He reveals. They are intimate with Him and are not distracted and don't take their focus away from following God. They understand the times and what they need to do.

Daniel is a man who read the Scriptures and thus understood the times. He understood the words of the prophet Jeremiah. He knew when it was time for the deliverance of

God's people. We've got to be people who read and understand the times. Philippians 3:7-17 is a powerful portion of Scripture:

> I once thought these things were valuable, but now I consider them worthless because of what Christ has done. Yes, everything else is worthless when compared with the infinite value of knowing Christ Jesus my Lord. For his sake I have discarded everything else, counting it all as garbage, so that I could gain Christ and become one with him. I no longer count on my own righteousness through obeying the law; rather, I become righteous through faith in Christ. For God's way of making us right with himself depends on faith. I want to know Christ and experience the mighty power that raised him from the dead. I want to suffer with him, sharing in his death, so that one way or another I will experience the resurrection from the dead!
>
> I don't mean to say that I have already achieved these things or that I have already reached perfection. But I press on to possess that perfection for which Christ Jesus first possessed me. No, dear brothers and sisters, I have not achieved it, but I focus on this one thing: Forgetting the past and looking forward to what lies ahead, I press on to reach the end of the race and receive the heavenly prize for which God, through Christ Jesus, is calling us. Let all who are spiritually mature agree on these things. If you disagree on some point, I believe God will make it plain to you.

Verse 16 is important: "But we must hold on to the progress we have already made." Paul said four things in all this that are important if we are to be able to move forward in this particular season.

Prior to this passage, Paul stated that he was a Jew of Jews, a Pharisee of Pharisees. He was at the school of Gamaliel, a well-known professor at the time. He was circumcised on the eighth day. Yet, Paul wrote that he counted all those distinctions as garbage. He left them behind. I'll come back to that again when I talk about leaving things behind, but he also wrote, "This is what I do now. I've counted all that is garbage. This is what I do." We must be like Paul and hold on to the progress we have made in the knowledge of God.

HOLDING ON TO YOUR PROGRESS

The first thing we must hold on to is our salvation. In Philippians 2:12, Paul had instructed them to work out their salvation with fear and trembling. We have received a Kingdom. We have received something precious from God and precious to God and it is the truth that has been passed to us. I think not only about the truth we have received but also the salvation, the promises of God, the dreams and goals in the Lord as we hold on in faithfulness of God, being faithful to the word of God in prayer, and holding on to the truth we have now.

When mentioning this, I'm reminded of Peter and the disciples when Jesus was crucified. They were losing hope. Peter suggested they go fishing. He was saying in essence, "This thing we've been doing was a disappointment, a failure. We've all been burned and misled." I would imagine Peter was very discouraged.

There could be reasons now for you to give up as well. We're not meeting the same way we had been meeting. We are not doing the same things we once did. Maybe you've experienced financial loss. Your church, maybe even the pastor, has not met your expectations and you are discouraged like Peter was.

What's the answer? Paul said hold on to the progress you have already made. We've made progress. People realized in the pandemic that money would not help them. Distractions and entertainment would not help them. People were reminded what was important and Paul said when you find those things, hold on to them and count everything else as worthless.

God has put treasures in your hands like your calling and the progress you have made toward it. You have the things and promises God has made to you and the things God has done. This is the time to remember the testimonies of God. Psalms 78 states that seeing that we have received the thing that our fathers have told us, those are the things to hold on to. Paul was saying that we should hold on to the progress we've made. So we hold on to our salvation and to the progress in our calling and understanding. The Kingdom of God is not in the building or other structures. The Kingdom of God is within us.

MISPLACED CONFIDENCE

The second point is found in verses seven and eight. Paul indicated there are worthless things in which we can place our confidence. We're at a place in the world where there's so much emphasis on how things look—the flesh, the pride of life, our achievements. That was true even for the church during the pandemic.

Megachurches and their buildings and programs were challenged. Some pastors have built their churches around their ministries and personalities. I'm not insinuating they're bad, but I'm saying God sent a message there that these things are not vital. God has shaken many things and we have found out how fragile they are but how indispensable God's presence and Word are. Before the pandemic, we were chasing after many things. Some of those things were not Kingdom values or matters. They were of no interest to or consistent with the values of God's Kingdom. We have had to recognize and reevaluate our priorities.

There's a story of an Italian tycoon who was sick, went to a hospital where he got well. When they told him how much he owed, he sobbed and cried loudly. The people in the hospital knew money was not a problem for this man. When he was able to explain himself, he said he realized how much it cost for him to have oxygen in the hospital when he had been breathing it for free all his life. For the first time in his life, he realized how valuable the oxygen was that he had taken for granted. It wasn't until he was deprived of that vital resource that he learned to appreciate it. The same is true for us during the pandemic. We realized what we had that we could no longer access and we realized its value.

Paul wrote about leaving things behind. Some have chosen relationships that are not godly. It's sad to see somebody walk away from God when they find a significant other. Paul urged us in these verses to reevaluate our lives to see where we are hanging on to worthless things. We sometimes put confidence in the flesh and some things which are not eternal. We put our confidence in what looks like achievement and success at the expense of much more important priorities. What are the things you will need to leave behind? Our priorities have got to be right now that we have come through this season.

KNOWING CHRIST

The third point is knowing Christ. Paul wrote, "That I may know Christ and the power of his resurrection, as well as the fellowship of his suffering." It came through loud and clear during the pandemic that we need to draw close to God and guard ourselves against fear, bitterness, and worry. We need to have God and draw near to Him.

I saw a clip of an address given years ago when a spiritual leader asked his audience, "What if all you would rely on is what you know on your own about God?" In other words, what if you had no priest or pastor but had to walk in the light of the knowledge you had? His second question was how much of the gospel would your children know if all they knew is what they have been taught at home?

We need to be more self-reliant and by that I mean we need to know Christ for ourselves. That was obvious during the pandemic since we did not have access to some of the spiritual resources and relationships to which we had become accustomed. People suddenly were stuck at home with their family and couldn't go to church. I know we had online services, but not everyone had that availability or were comfortable with that opportunity.

My point is that knowing Christ on a personal level was shown to be vitally important. That is what Paul wrote: "I want to know him, to know Christ personally, be associated with him, intimate with Him." We need an intimacy with Christ in this time. How can we move forward? We'll move forward through an intimate relationship with God when we know Him personally.

I'm reminded of the book of Daniel 11:32: "Those that do wickedness will continue in wickedness but they that know their God, they will be strong and do exploits." We will see and perform exploits as we're moving forward. It's those who know God and have an intimate relationship with Him who will see the Kingdom. They will make up the remnant I mentioned earlier. The forceful people lay hold of it. These people are intimate with God and seek God. They will move forward and advance.

PRESSING FORWARD

The fourth point is when Paul talked about pressing forward. He said he was pressing to perfection, to reach up and move on. There is a race that we must run. Those who move forward must realize there is a race which has an eternal focus. We should not be scared. Paul said for him to live is Christ and to die is gain. He saw that to be absent from this body is to be present with Christ. We are not perfect but moving forward.

Don't be discouraged. Press on to the mark, to the eternal goal, living a life where the word of God dwells richly in you. It is Christ in us who is the hope of glory while we keep our focus on eternal life. Evaluate where you are in relationship to the areas we have previewed in this chapter. We talked about holding on to the wisdom of the things we've received; about evaluating our lives; about knowing Christ and having an intimate relationship with God; about pressing on and looking to and having an eternal focus of life.

We've heard the saying that we can be so heavenly minded that we are of no earthly good. At the same time, sometimes we are so earthly that we are no heavenly good. I am not talking about being perfect. Paul stated he was not perfect, but he was pressing on to the higher call of God in Christ. He was pressing on through faith to Jesus. You need to do the same. You can progress and move forward. How do you do that? You move by grace, depending on it and by faith. You press on by finding and then holding on to the truth, to the things that you have received. That's how we're going to move forward.

5

WE WILL NOT BOW

I received this message as a prophetic word during the time of the pandemic but it has relevance now in the days immediately following as well. It's good to understand God's purpose at this time. We must be alert and awake. Looking at the book of Daniel, let me explain God's word for this period of time which begins with us understanding God's purpose.

The word of God declares in the book of Romans 8:28 that all things work together for good for them who love the Lord and are called according to His purpose. You may ask me what was and is God's purpose in this season. In Acts 17, there's an interesting portion of Scripture that covers part of Paul's second missionary journey, which was to have run between A.D. 49 to A.D. 52. In that period of time, he traveled through Asia Minor, across the Mediterranean, and into Athens, Greece, and Macedonia.

In Acts 17, Paul was in Athens. As he was going through Athens, he saw several altars. One of the altars had an inscription "to an unknown god." After that Paul went before the Epicureans, the philosophers, and the council of the city to present his gospel. The Greeks loved to debate in the town hall or the meeting places of the city. This is where Paul met the Epicureans and Stoics who were the philosophers of their day. He engaged them intellectually and philosophically there. Paul told them he had seen the altar to the unknown god and told them about this God they were worshiping without knowledge. In Acts 17:24-27 Paul said,

> "He is the God who made the world and everything in it. Since he is Lord of heaven and earth, he doesn't live in man-made temples, and human hands can't serve his needs—for he has no needs. He himself gives life and breath to everything, and he satisfies every need. From one man he created all the nations throughout the whole earth. He decided beforehand when they should rise and fall, and he determined their boundaries. His purpose was for the nations to seek after God and perhaps feel their way toward him and find him—though he is not far from any one of us."

"He is not far from any one of us." That's an important statement. Paul expanded this truth for them because he saw the purpose of God. God created all nations. He determined their rise to prominence and their downfall. Then he stated that God's purpose was for people to seek and find Him. He has made that possible through the Christ Paul preached. During the pandemic, God's ultimate and number one purpose was that people should seek and find Him. It's important for us to recognize that.

SEEK AND FIND HIM

God's first purpose was that people should seek and find Him. His second purpose is found in Ephesians 3:10: "God's purpose in all this was to use a church to display his wisdom in its rich variety, to all the unseen rulers and authorities in the heavenly places." God's purpose and intent were to display

His wisdom. It states in another translation *manifold wisdom*. The beauty of it all is that God displays His splendor and wisdom through the Church to the unseen principalities and to earthly kingdoms. This is an important point to note of which we need to be aware.

We saw that in the recent crisis we have just gone through, many regulations and much legislation were put into effect because of COVID. Now it's important to obey authority for all authority comes from God. However, when the authority goes against the will and purpose of God, we have a legitimate reason for disobeying that authority. I'll give you the example from the life of Daniel.

The authority stated it was illegal to pray. Daniel did not obey the authority because that authority was setting up regulations contrary to the will and purpose of God. The same would hold true today. Any authority that sets itself up against the Church is not legitimate. When that happens and the Church resists, then the Church usually faces persecution. The early Church certainly did. In the early Church, Peter said that the authorities should not decide whether the disciples should obey them or God. The disciples chose to obey God and disobey the order they were given not to preach or teach about Jesus.

As we hear edicts or declarations, it's important that we as a church walk in wisdom. Any wisdom that is not in line with the Word of God, that goes contrary to the Word, contradicts God's purpose. Those directives we cannot obey. We shouldn't bow to any entity that is not in line with the will and purpose of God. Our primary command is to fear God and not to fear man, to obey his commands and to obey his word. That is our primary purpose as believers and Christians.

During this time, it's important we be alert. There is a lot to hear and the Bible says he who has an ear to hear, let him hear what the Spirit is saying to the Church. We should also be alert to see because we live in a world of technology. A lot of things are happening that we should see. We see trends of which we should be conscious and clear as to their meaning and destination. There's an interesting portion of scripture in the book of Ephesians 3:1-5:

> When I think of all of this, I, Paul, a prisoner of Christ Jesus for the benefit of the Gentiles, assuming by way that, God gave me the special responsibility of extending his grace to you Gentiles. As I briefly wrote earlier, God himself revealed his mysterious plan to me. As you read what I have written, you will understand my insight into the plan regarding Christ. God did not reveal it to previous generations, but now by the spirit, he has revealed it to his holy apostles and prophets.

In other words, God has revealed His mystery. The point I'm trying to make here is that God will reveal His mysteries to His servants—apostles and prophets. Even in this season and time, God reveals His mysteries. The Bible says God does nothing without revealing it to his servants, the prophets (see Amos 3:7). The topic in this chapter is "Don't Bow" so let me explain that title as taken from Daniel 3.

In an overview of Daniel 3, we see Shadrach, Meshach, and Abednego, the three Hebrew boys, who were members of the king's advisory team, having to choose between loyalty to the Kingdom of God and the kingdom of Babylon represented by King Nebuchadnezzar. Naturally, they chose allegiance to the Kingdom of God and they refused to bow.

DON'T BOW

That's why I titled this chapter "Don't Bow." Are we in a period when we are likely going to be in situations where we will have to choose between the Kingdom of God and the kingdom of darkness? I think we are. The Church is not going to have an easy time of it, for we are going to have to choose between the dark kingdom, and the Kingdom of God. In Daniel 3:1-6, we read

> King Nebuchadnezzar made a gold statue 90 feet tall and 80 feet wide. And set it up in the plain of Dura in the province of Babylon. Then he sent messages to hire officers, officials, governors, advices, treasurers, judges, magistrates, and all the provincial officials to come to the dedication of this statue he had set up. All these officials all came and

> stood before the statue of Nebuchadnezzar he had set up. Then a herald shouted out, people of all races and nations and languages listen to the King's command. When you hear the sound of the flute, zither, liar, pipes, and other musical instruments about the grounds, worship King Nebuchadnezzar's gold statue. Anyone who refuses to will immediately be thrown into a blazing furnace. At the sound of musical instruments, all the people, whatever nation, or language, bowed to the ground, worshiped the gold statue that King Nebuchadnezzar had set up.

Then in Daniel 3:13, 15, 20 and 24, we see

> Then Nebuchadnezzar flew into rage and ordered that Shadrach, Meshach, and Abednego be brought before him. When they were brought in, he said, "I will give you one more chance to bow down and worship the statue I have made when you hear the sound of the musical instruments. If you refuse, you will be thrown immediately into blazing finance, and then what God will be able to rescue you from my power?" . . . Shadrach, Meshach, and Abednego replied, "Oh Nebuchadnezzar, we did not need to defend ourselves before you. If we are thrown into the blazing furnace the God whom we serve is able to save us. He will rescue us from your power your Majesty, but even if he doesn't, we want to make it clear to you, you might just see that we will never serve your gods or worship the gold statue that you have set up." . . . Then that's when he ordered some of the strongest men of his to bind Shadrach, Meshach, and Abednego and throw them into the blazing furnace.

Then we read in Daniel 3:24-30,

> But suddenly Nebuchadnezzar jumped up in amazement and exclaimed to his advisors. "Didn't we tie the three men and throw them into the furnace?" "Yes, your Majesty, we certainly did." Then

> Nebuchadnezzar shouted, "I see four men, unbound walking around in the fire, unharmed and the fourth looks like a God." Then Nebuchadnezzar said, "Praise to the God of Shadrach, Meshach, and Abednego. He sent an angel to rescue his servant who trusted in him. They defied the King's command and were willing to die rather than serve or worship any God except their God." Then Nebuchadnezzar promoted Shadrach, Meshach, and Abednego to even higher positions in the province of Babylon.

Let's look at some additional historical background for this event. Nebuchadnezzar had conquered Jerusalem and Judah. This was part of his expansion as he continued to build the city of Babylon and his kingdom. Babylon was an elaborate place with many gods, statues, and public works. They continued to build a magnificent culture that followed the pattern and humanistic spirit of the Tower of Babel. The word *babel* meant "connecting heaven and a gateway to God as the stairway to heaven."

In John's gospel, Jesus declared He is the stairway to heaven, but Babylon's system was one of self-exaltation, where the people and leaders sought to be exalted and raised above the heavens. It's a system of power, control, and knowledge advancement, which started with the tower of Babel where God caused people to be confused, unable to understand one another. This happened in the land of Ur of the Chaldeans. It's important to note these things because God took Abraham out of this land and said that from him the nations of the earth would be blessed.

Babylon and Babel represent a system without God—an anti-Christ spirit. It is out of this corrupt system that God chose a man named Abraham and used him to create, establish, and continue His purpose on the earth through His own nation. It was out of him and this nation that all nations of the earth would be blessed.

The prophets proclaimed that ruined Babylon would never be rebuilt after it was completely destroyed. That prophecy has held true and Babylon is still in ruins today, never to be rebuilt. (You can find that in Jeremiah 50:2,and Isaiah 13:17-20 regarding the destruction and the ruins of the Babylon.) God did this because Babylon was a corrupt system that set itself up against God.

I drew a number of lessons from those verses in Daniel 3. The first one is we should not and will not bow. Second, there was a fourth man in the fire. Then, we see the promotion of Shadrach, Meshach, Abednego. The final lesson is in the context of Jesus' coming back and the time in which we're living right now, especially in light of the pandemic. Let's look at each one of these lessons more closely.

1. THEY DID NOT BOW

In Daniel 3:18, the three men said to the king, "Be it known to you King, we will not bow. We will not bow to your dictates, we will not bow to the things of foreign gods, or this corrupt system." They had to choose between serving and worshiping God or not.

In this period as we move forward, one of the things that is going to be clear is that there are going to be situations where we must distinguish our response of whether to worship God or not. Do we serve God? Do we bow down? Do we bow to worship other gods when economics is involved? When there's money or choices that are social in nature, do we bow? When there are choices that are in line with modern values but against those in God's word, do we bow? The three young men made a choice that they were not going to bow regardless of the consequences. That was a decision made in faith.

They said they knew their God was able to deliver them, but even if He chose not to deliver them from the flames, they would not bow. There may be times or situations as we are only moving forward that we have got to make a choice. Are we going to be like Shadrach, Meshack, and Abednego, or are we going to bow down?

2. A FOURTH MAN

As a result of their choice, we are told in verse 24 that there were four men, unbound and walking around in the fire. What's more, the fourth looked like a god. We know this fourth man was what's called a Christophany where God appears as man. In the Old Testament, whenever God appeared as man, we know it was Jesus. The fourth man, appeared and saved them from the fire. Jesus protected them and they were not harmed.

Jesus was the fourth man in the fire because He is the connector and intermediary between heaven and earth. He's the rescuer. He will always come to the rescue of His own people. Jesus said He is the stairway to God and heaven in John 1:51: "I tell you the truth. You will see the heaven open again. You will see it open and the angels of God going up and down on the son of man." Jesus is the fourth man who will protect His people, doing what the tower of Babel or any other world system cannot possibly do.

3. GOD'S HELP

When Nebuchadnezzar saw the fourth man, he said, "Praise to the God of Shadrach, Meshach, and Abednego. He sent his angel to rescue his servants who trusted in him that defied the King's command and were willing to die rather than serve or worship any God, except their God." God came and rescued them, and Nebuchadnezzar saw it.

During the pandemic as I was seeking God, one of the things that clearly came as a word to me is that God is going to show Himself. I had a vision of a stairway between heaven and earth. Just like Meshach, Shadrach, and Abednego, the people of God are going to make a stand and take a position that honors God and as a result, God is going to show Himself strong on their behalf. God is going to come through for His people no matter what trial. This is a time we are going to see God. I remind you that in the book of Chronicles 16:9, it says, "For the eyes of the Lord run to and fro and throughout the whole earth." He must show Himself strong on their behalf.

Isaiah 40:28 says that He gives power to the weak and to those who have no might, He increases strength. Paul wrote that when he was weak, he was really quite strong (see 2 Corinthians 12:9). The point is that when His people take a stand for Him, as we see with Meshach, Shadrach, and Abednego, God is going to show Himself strong on their behalf. This is the word of God. This time will be like the time of Daniel in Babylon. God will show himself strong on behalf of his people.

4. A TIME OF PROMOTION

God promoted the three men as recorded in Daniel 3:30. Consider the fact that earlier the report was that there were certain Jews in Babylon who were of no consequence. They meant nothing. They were not bowing. It turns out they did have significance after all in the eyes of God. The outcome of the event elevated them from being insignificant to having exalted names. They were promoted.

Prophetically let me say this. Voices are going to emerge that have not been heard before because of the pandemic. Some ministries that were insignificant are going to become significant. Those voices are being raised in these times. We may miss or not recognize these voices because they are emerging from unfamiliar places and sources, not the big churches, ministries, or teachers we have known. As we move forward during this period, God is promoting ministries and people from insignificant places to places of significance just like He did with the three men.

5. THE END TIMES

It's important we see the pandemic period in the context of the end times. We are nearing the time when Jesus is coming back. It says in Matthew 24:14, "For nation will rise against nation and kingdom against kingdom, and there will be famines, and pestilences, and earthquakes in various places." In these days, famines have been many. There has been an increase of earthquakes, pestilence, plagues (some versions actually add epidemics), and diseases.

The Word also says that false prophets would rise up. In Matthew 24:7, we learn that "nation will go against nation and kingdom against kingdom and there will be famines, and earthquakes in many parts of the world." The good news of the Kingdom will be preached throughout the whole world. All the nations will hear it. These are signs the end is near and the Lord is coming back.

The question is: Are you, are we, ready? Are you ready

for the coming of Jesus? Are you prepared for the coming of Jesus? That's something that I will leave you to think about. Are you prepared? We need to be prepared to be the bride. He will protect her through it all. He will protect them through whatever is coming.

6

RETURN TO GOD

"He that has an ear to hear, let him hear what the Spirit of the Lord says." That admonition was uttered to every church addressed in the first four chapters of Revelation. In view of the times we are living in, it's important that we hear what the Spirit of the Lord is saying to the Church. Even if you are not a believer, I urge you to heed what I'm telling you for there is a time when you will need this message or wish you had heeded it.

The message is quite simply return to God. God is quoted in Second Chronicles 7:13 as saying, "I will shut heavens, and there will be no rain fall. I will command grasshoppers to devour the crops of the field or send plagues among you." Then He promised, "If my people who are called by my name will humble themselves and pray and seek my face and turn from their wicked ways, then I will hear from heaven, I will forgive their sins. I will restore their lands" (2 Chronicles 7:14). Note the word he uses: "I will restore their lands."

In other words, when God's people turn back to God

in prayer and repentance, He will hear and bring healing and restoration. It doesn't matter whether it's a nation or an individual, God's mercy endures forever as do His promises. David prayed, "Have mercy on me according to your everlasting love" (Psalm 51:1) which speaks of God's restorative grace.

Then in Joel 2:25, we read, "I will restore what the canker worm has eaten. I will restore what the palmer worm has eaten." In other words, God says to His people that He is a restoring God who will come to them and restore them and their land. That "land" has many facets and may be economic, physical, or social. Restoration means He will not only reinstate things to their previous state but He will also bring His people to a better state. He rejuvenates and renews them.

God encourages us to have knowledge and understanding of what He is doing in our situation and circumstances. He wants us to have wisdom and to discern what is happening. When we have that sort of understanding, then we can walk in a way that is pleasing to God. We can walk in alignment with what God is doing and saying. Then we are able to enter into that restorative place and space. We are able to move then and even take advantage of the opportunities being presented to us despite the adversity we are seeing. This is especially true now at this time of the pandemic recovery. There's a need to have understanding of God's promises and heart.

This chapter is an encouragement but it also contains a word of caution. We must develop the right attitudes if we are going to move forward so we can align with what God is doing and saying. That way we will not miss the opportunity being created. Let me address how we will get back to normal when we start to emerge from this.

What will happen? How do we go from that position from the lockdown when the church is restored and we're able to travel again and freely move about again? I don't want to miss what God is doing in the next move of God into which we are headed.

UNDERSTANDING THE TIMES

First, I want to paint a picture of the times in which we are living. After that, I will give you a word of caution. Then

I will list three things we need to do that will help us move forward. Let me start to bring an understanding of where we are today based on the Old Testament book of Daniel as I have done in previous chapters. You can see that Daniel has occupied my time and attention in this season. If you want to understand the events of today, you should go to Daniel and Revelation. Jesus talked about the same in Matthew 24 and in Luke 17. They all give us a picture of where we are.

The pandemic didn't just happen. Such things were predicted. We serve an omniscient and all-knowing God who knows yesterday, today, and the future. A song says because He lives, I can face tomorrow. There is a truth in that. Because He lives, He holds our future in His hands. It doesn't matter where you are. It doesn't matter what your condition is. You should be encouraged that God holds the future.

For example in 1986, He brought His word through a servant of God by the name of David Wilkerson who wrote *The Cross and the Switchblade*. In that book, he predicted that a pandemic would hit New York like never before. It's no wonder we saw what happened in New York. He predicted that something unusual would hit New York. That was back in 1986 and today we are seeing that New York has been devastated by the coronavirus.

We read in 1 Thessalonians 5:2-4 that the end will come as a thief but there is yet another thing Paul wrote. He reminded us that we are not in darkness so that the day should not surprise us like a thief would. As a believer, God's idea is for us to understand His will. Jesus said, "My meat is to do the will of Him who sent me" (John 4:34). He could do this because He understood what His Father was doing. He understood what was happening in the world. He did exactly what was necessary from that point in time. Now that we have Him living in us, we should know and then do the same as He did—understand and be relevant for the times in which we live. Let's look at Daniel 2:36-45

> "That was the dream. Now he will tell the king what it means. Your Majesty, you are the greatest of kings, the God of heaven has given you Serenity,

power, strength, and honor. He has made you the ruler of all the inhabited world. He has put even the wild animals and birds under your control. You are the head of gold. But after your kingdom comes to an end another kingdom inferior to yours will rise to take your place and after that kingdom has fallen yet a third kingdom represented by bronze will rise to rule the world. Following that kingdom there will be a fourth one as strong as iron and that kingdom will smash and crush the previous empires. Just as iron smashes and crushes everything it strikes. The feet and toes are a combination of iron baked with clay showing that this kingdom will be divided like iron mixed with clay. It will have some of the strength of iron though. While some of it will be strong as iron other parts will be as weak as clay. This mixture of iron and clay shows that this kingdom will try to strengthen themselves by forming alliances with each other through intermarriage, but they will not hold together just as iron and clay do not mix. During the reigns of those kings the God of heaven will set up a kingdom that will never be destroyed or conquered. It will crush all these kingdoms into nothing, and it will stand forever. That is the meaning of the rock cut from the mountain, though not by human hands that crushed into pieces the statue of iron, bronze and clay, silver, and gold. The great God was showing the king what will happen in the future. The dream is true, and its meaning is sudden. In other words, the dream is true, and it will happen suddenly, just as has been told."

King Nebuchadnezzar ruled Babylon, and was the king of the Chaldeans. He had a dream one night and saw a huge shining statue of man with a head of gold, chest and arms of silver, the belly and thighs of bronze, legs of iron, and the feet a combination of iron and baked clay. A rock was cut from a mountain but not by human hands and struck the feet of the statue, smashing it to bits. The statue was then crushed into fine pieces. The wind blew away the iron and clay and silver and bronze and gold.

We pick up the story from the interpretation. Even before that, we were told that the king called the astrologers, soothsayers, and magicians in the royal court for an interpretation. He demanded the interpretation but refused to tell them the dream. If they couldn't tell him the interpretation, he threatened to tear them limb from limb. If anyone could reveal the meaning, they would receive great honor.

Later in chapter seven, by the way, Daniel had a dream of his own and God explained to him exactly what it meant and what was going to happen. God revealed that it was about kingdoms that would be established in this world. We need to understand this lesson for it pertains to world affairs and what is happening now. Now let's look at what Daniel told the King.

"King, this is what it is. The head is you. The head of gold is your kingdom and that is the kingdom of Babylon. You are a powerful and mighty king. There will be a kingdom that will come after you." We know that the kingdom of Babylon was conquered by the kingdom of the Medes and Persians. The kingdom after that was Greece that conquered the kingdom of Persia, led by the powerful Alexander the Great.

THE KINGDOMS

After that, Greece was conquered by the kingdom of Rome which ruled from about 500 B.C. to about 500 A.D., almost a thousand years. After Rome, the kingdom was divided which was represented in the dream by iron mixed with clay. I still remember my Western Civilization Professor, Dr. Polonsky at Columbia College in Missouri, telling us that just like the Bible said, Rome suddenly fell and it didn't know what hit it. The rock described in Daniel hit it.

God was showing Daniel world affairs starting with Babylon. God had placed Daniel in the government there so he could reveal matters about kingdoms in the future. God has a way of placing us in settings so we can understand the systems we are in from a Kingdom perspective. May I encourage you to understand because as you will see shortly, God wants and needs us to have understanding, wisdom, and knowledge.

What was the message of Jesus when He came? He said repent for the Kingdom of God has come. When God spoke to Adam and Eve, He told Adam to reign and have dominion. After Adam failed and fell, God allowed kings to reign and have control. Man raised up alternative kingdoms that have not aligned with the will of God or established His Kingdom rule.

Remember that a stone was predicted that would come and hit the statue portrayed in the king's dream with Daniel. God's Kingdom was the stone that came and hit Rome and nobody knew what hit it. It was no longer the single most powerful world kingdom. The British, Germans, Spanish, and many others have established kingdoms since. In reality, they are just fragments of the former Roman Empire.

There are only two nations or kingdoms: God's kingdom and those in rebellion to that Kingdom. Because man is a spiritual being, man will worship something. An example of this is what happened after Daniel interpreted the dream. King Nebuchadnezzar made a statue and tried to make sure that Shadrach, Meshack, and Abednego worshiped it. Of course, they didn't.

When the king wanted to kill the astrologers, magicians, and those in the court for not being able to interpret his dream, Daniel stepped in and interpreted it for him, saving all the wise men. He in faith declared that the God of heaven was going to give him understanding so he could interpret, which he did. That's how he saved all the officials including his friends Shadrach, Meshack, and Abednego.

Let me digress for a moment and share some insight I believe the Lord gave me about what I refer to as alternative forms of worship. There are two churches that took on the name of one of the world's great empires. The first is the Roman church that formed the Holy Roman Empire and the other is the Church of England.

Rome joined forces with the spiritual rulers of Jesus' day to condemn Him to death through its criminal justice system. Then when Emperor Constantine reigned from 306 through 337, he actually became a Christian and the Church and the government became one in the sense that people were forced into believing. Roman Emperors Constantine and Licinius signed the Edict of Milan, which declared tolerance for Christianity after the persecution of Christians under Nero and other emperors. Then centuries later, there were the Crusades, again officially sponsored by the State and papacy.

The point I want you to see is the phenomenon of how the Church and State merged to form a religion. Rather than the king aligning and using God's statutes to rule, we see an alignment of the Church with secular rulers. These became world kingdoms and not godly kingdoms.

We saw a similar thing when King Saul came to power after the Israelites demanded God give them a king like the other kingdoms had. We know that King Saul became the king, but he did many wrong things and moved away from God until God replaced him with a king named David, son of Jesse, a man after God's heart. God promised David that his kingdom would and shall not come to an end for Jesus was to be a son of David.

OUR TIMES

Let's go back to Daniel and examine the end of this story to help us understand the times we are in. There are four points. First, it's about control of the earth. In Daniel 2:38, God told Daniel to inform the king that He had given him power over the animals and birds, along with power and authority to control the earth, the same mandate that was given to Adam to be fruitful and multiply and have dominion. Adam was supposed to do it by obeying God and His Word but he was deceived so God removed Adam and Eve from the garden of Eden for not doing things God's way.

Over the years that rebellion has continued through anti-God alternative governments and movements. When David came on the scene, God told him that He would establish from his descendants another king like him, a man who would rule according to the dictates of God's law. That man is Jesus Christ the King of Kings who came out of the lineage of David, humanly speaking, to regain control.

That's important because a lot of things will go wrong. Why did things go wrong? Why do we have war in Syria?

Why do we have the pandemic? There are a lot of things in the pandemic that are as a result of man's efforts to rule in the place of God. For a season, God allows humans to have control of things. He lets them do things on earth with authority, power, and the control He's given. When they do that, things happen as a result of man making decisions that are not according to God's will. There is a saying that God made man, man made money, money made man mad. So point number one is that according to Daniel, God had given the king control.

Jesus came to establish God's kingdom which will never be destroyed. God promises redemption from all oppressive powers that oppose God. The rock hewn from the mountain will strike the statue and destroy the other kingdoms. Therefore, we can move forward, doing what we need to do because we belong to the Kingdom of God that will ultimately annihilate the other kingdoms. It may for a moment look like it won't happen, but I reassure you that God will do it.

That then brings me to another prophetic word. What does God require you to do? Remember that word of God in the book of Micah? "I have shown you, oh man, what is good and what the Lord requires of thee" (Micah 6:8). What does God require of us in the context of COVID now and moving forward? How would God want us to lead? What are the instructions? What does God require of us now?

INTIMACY WITH HIM

There are three things that if we do them, we will return to God and then the blessings will abound. What does God require of us in this time? The first is intimacy with God, a personal knowledge of and relating to God as never before. If there's any time that you need to be close to God, it's right now.

One of the words closely associated with intimacy is obedience. The Bible tells us that obedience is better than sacrifice. Obedience means following the law of God. God will crush the rebellion that began in the Garden of Eden, that continued until the time of Noah, and was seen in the building of the Tower of Babel. God is going to deal with that rebellion finally in the lake of fire, the end of the antichrist, which is rebellion against God. That includes any so-called secular new world order and any such "innovation" outside of God.

Another word associated with intimacy is purity. In marriage, purity is being faithful. Another word associated with intimacy is humility. The Bible says to "humble yourself before the Lord and He will lift you up" (1 Peter 5:6). Another word tied to intimacy is submission. As a wife submits to her husband, we should submit to God and to one another. It means being under the authority of and honouring God as He controls your life and assigns delegated authority to represent Him as authorities over you.

Another word is sanctification or holiness. You don't hear much about these words in the Church today. Part of the problem is that secularism has been encroaching upon the Church. The music, instead of being spiritual, is often secular. Sanctification and holiness mean integrity, genuineness of heart, being honest as to what's in your heart. The same person you portray on the outside is actually the same person you are on the inside in your secret place.

Trust is related to intimacy and means you trust God in everything and don't lean on your own understanding. Another word associated with intimacy is truthfulness. Be honest and truthful. Let your yes be yes and your no be no. So the first thing you need to establish and cultivate in this season is intimacy with the Lord and with other believers. Finally, the last word is worship.

God will not settle for second place in your life. God is either first or He is last; there is no in between. God will not be second to your job. He will not be second to your children. He will not be second to your spouse. God is either first or He is not God of your life. God is a jealous God. You must not worship another thing. That's what the apostles had. They were killed. They died because they left everything.

Jesus once asked Peter when people were abandoning Jesus if Peter wanted to leave too. Peter responded that they had left everything to follow Him, so they had no place else to go. Jesus then said, "Whoever leaves one's husband, or one's wife, whoever leaves everything and comes to me will be blessed and will receive in this world one hundred fold and in the world to come eternal life." In other words, we will live in this Kingdom here and will live in the Kingdom that is forever. Amen.

The second thing God requires now is meaningful and godly relationships. We talk of relationships and building relationships with one another. Jesus gave His commandment that said He was giving us a new commandment to love one another. It was really just an old commandment. We are to love our neighbor and one another. COVID-19 showed us that relationships are vital. We have to maintain relationships with family and friends and with our church family, relationships that matter and bring life. We are to make amends if we think of someone with whom we have had a falling out. It's not a time to be bitter and away from other people.

Terms associated with relationships are care, kindness, and a sense of belonging. Identify those relationships that matter and keep those relationships. During the pandemic, I reconnected with some I hadn't been connected to for a long time. I also connected with many new friends and associates.

As we close, let me add one more thing or rather a collection of things we need in this season: knowledge, understanding, and wisdom. Knowledge involves knowing the truth about the facts. Get new information that's the right information. When you know the truth, it will set you free. Don't be deceived because in the last days deception will increase. How do you prevent deception? You conquer it by having the right knowledge.

The other word is understanding. You must move beyond knowing facts to understanding systems. Understand the systems of this world and how they work. How does the government work? How does the economy work? How does His Kingdom work in you? God wants to raise you up. The Bible says those who know their God will be strong and do exploits.

There's going to be a revival. We are going to see people coming into the Kingdom because everything has been shaken or is going to be shaken. People are going to run to God. People are already running to God. Those people need others who know how to help them.

And finally, there is wisdom which is the correct application of knowledge and understanding—knowing what to do and when to do. Knowing when to open your mouth and when to shut it. Wisdom is knowing how to relate to people so you can keep relationships. The Bible says in Proverbs 9:10, "The fear or God is the beginning of all wisdom." That speaks of returning to God. The pandemic is a wake-up call to the Church and humanity to return to God.

7

THE MURDER OF GEORGE FLOYD

I want to weigh in on the matter of George Floyd and what went on in the U.S. with the riots and protests in 2020 and beyond. Just like others, you may have felt the correct response or emotion was anger. That was and is the inclination of many people because we are emotional beings. However, I'm reminded of what Paul wrote in his letter to the Ephesians 4:26 "Be angry, but don't sin by letting anger control you. Don't let the sun go down while you are still angry."

Two things are important to keep in mind as we examine the emotion of anger. One is that we shouldn't let anger control us. I'm talking particularly to Christians and God's people. I'm aware that young people and children are affected by these events and it's important that we teach them properly through our example and our words. As parents, we can help our children process events like these so we can protect them from anger that could consume them. The first thing we see that Paul wrote is not to sin by allowing anger or our emotions to control us.

The second part of what he wrote is that we are not to let the anger linger or live on. The only way to get around this is to forgive. Jesus taught us to do that in prayer, which is found in what is not really the Lord's Prayer, but our prayer. We need to forgive and vocalize that we have done so. That's why it's an element of prayer to speak or declare that we have forgiven. That is the essence of the phrase "forgive us our trespasses, as we forgive those who trespass against us."

I'm also reminded of the Serenity Prayer written by Reinhold Niebuhr in 1932, the first part of which states, "God give me the grace to accept, with serenity, the things that cannot be changed, courage to change the things which should be changed, and the wisdom to distinguish the one from the other." This is also important. We need the grace to realize and accept the things we are unable to change.

I'm writing this message because I'm hoping I can influence the mind of somebody by releasing this message in obedience to God, hoping that there are some who will do something right. A lawyer could go to court. Activists could make a phone call. A minister could preach a message and explain this to the people. There are things we must do at this time. If we don't, then bad things happen when good people do nothing. There are times when we have got to do something.

It is possible to change somebody's perspective. When we have that opportunity, we should go ahead and do it. However, according to the prayer, we should have the grace, with serenity, to accept the things that cannot be changed. Developing the wisdom to distinguish between what can and can't be changed is very important.

In this season, I want to emphasize the power of prayer. You may not have a platform to speak, but prayer is very powerful. It reminds me again of a situation in Daniel's life. Daniel found himself in a difficult situation in Daniel 9:1-4:

It was the first year in the reign of Darius, the

> Mede, the son of Ahasuerus who became King of Babylon, during the first year of this reign, I Daniel, had learned from the reading the word of the Lord, as revealed to Jeremiah, the prophet, that Jerusalem might be desolate for 70 years. So, I turned to the Lord God and pleaded with him in prayer and fasting. I also wore rough burlap and sprinkled myself with ashes. I prayed to the Lord, my God, and confessed.

Let me break this passage down. Daniel understood the need of the moment. He understood that information was and is important. He read the word of God and so he understood the time and what was happening. The book of Jeremiah was a historical record so Daniel understood what had been said and applied it to his own day. He understood the connection and consequently went to God in prayer.

Notice that Daniel took personal responsibility. He took it upon himself to confess his sins and the sins of his people. God sent an answer explaining what was happening and what was going to happen in that present time and in the future, but it started with repentance and confession. This is how God makes known His secrets.

When we pray, God communicates with and reveals things to us. God gives an understanding of His timing and secrets. The only way we will have access to the secrets of heaven—to the will and purpose of God—is by prayer. That reminds me of Psalms 25:14, which says, "The secret of the Lord is with those who fear him. He will show them his covenant." God reveals to us so we can understand the times we live in.

In these times of COVID-19, it is only through prayer and calling on God that we can clearly understand the times in which we live. As a result, we can then understand how we are to live and respond in a time like this.

Let me finish by saying this, especially concerning George Floyd and the racial issues that have been going on in the world for a long time. It's easy to get emotional about these incidents. Keep in mind, however, that we are dealing with sin. We're also dealing with the system of injustice and evil first hatched in the garden of Eden and it has gone on for many years and centuries whether we're talking about poverty, injustice, or the unfairness inherent in the systems of this world. Only God will be able to address and deal with it all for it is truly monumental. Only He can and will finally address and deal with it. As a child of God, I encourage you to remain focused on God and His Kingdom. That means that you behave as God would have you to do.

8

MESSAGE TO THE DIASPORA

In this chapter, I address what some may consider a sensitive subject, one that is taboo to discuss. Nevertheless, it's an important one. It's a particularly important topic with regard to ministry among or with Africans, whatever the case may be. Often in our fellowships with interracial relationships or in multicultural contexts, we gloss over these matters or behave without sensitivity and in ways that obviously perpetuate polarizing perspectives or unhelpful racial attitudes. It's only when something major happens, such as the George Floyd murder, that the issues come to the forefront and are discussed, albeit inconclusively because as I have said, they are taboo to talk about.

I understand the divisive nature of DMins around race but also not being open to discussing these issues is one of the problems of interracial relationships. I also think that certain racially-oriented attitudes and behaviours from either sides of the divide or debate emerge from ignorance and a lack of understanding. This chapter has a specific message to my fellow Africans in the Diaspora.

The African Diaspora is broadly defined by the African Union Commission as "peoples of African origin living outside the continent, irrespective of their citizenship and nationality and who are willing to contribute to the development of the continent and the building of the African Union." Globally, Africans in the Diaspora are spread out across the continents. In North America, there are 39 million from the African Diaspora; 13 million in Latin America; 13.6 million in the Caribbean; and 3.5 million in Europe, the World Bank estimates.

Beyond politics and economics, I believe that Africans in the Diaspora can be greatly impactful if they understand God's purpose and will for humanity. Not only are the perceived attitudes of others (discrimination) important in this DMin, but also our own as I begin with a description of the "Dark Continent" concept. The label *dark continent* originated among "imperialist" European leaders that colonized parts of Africa but also led to subsequent campaigns to end slavery. At that time, this was seen as the need and justification for missionary work.

However, these events and subsequent engagements with the continent of Africa ignored certain parts of the continent's history while at the same perpetuating stereotypes and false images of African history. We may assume racism does not exist, or racial thinking does not affect the way we do church, because we purport to have a Kingdom culture.

However, it requires more than a day to build or change culture, so establishing a Kingdom culture doesn't happen in one night. It involves the renewal of the mind and putting off the old man while putting on the new. It also involves learning to live according to the dictates of the new being that now exists in and through Christ Jesus, bought by His blood and transformed into the full stature of Christ Jesus.

I once read a book which presented a radical concept

of what the author called "colonizability" (*colonisabilité* in French). The author maintained that the French presence in Algeria started a process there that caused the culture not to improve but rather to decline to a stage where colonizing became necessary. That enabled them to colonize the country. He referred to the concept as colonizability.

The author made a distinction between a country that is conquered and occupied and one that is colonized. He claimed a country that is colonized loses its own cultural bearing and then internalizes the idea that the colonizing culture is superior to the local existing one.

One important thing to draw out from his premise is the distinction between a country that is conquered or occupied and one that is colonized. A country that is colonized loses its own cultural bearing and then internalizes the idea of the superiority of the colonizing culture.

Let me give you an example from my own experience. In my home country of Kenya, if you are white and use a matatu or large van for transportation, people are surprised because they think a white man is superior and isn't supposed to be riding in a *matatu* or any public transport. If they see a white man walking barefoot, they would be surprised. Why? Because the white man is superior and isn't supposed to be doing that.

Expanding on that, we would look at a white person and expect them to have a lot of money simply because they are white. It is part of the thinking that the other culture or citizens in that culture are superior because we have been taught and conditioned to think that way.

This thinking can also exist in a church by means of a leadership style that treats some as inferior to others and it can exist at a subconscious level. No one is aware that it exists and is affecting decisions. It's important that we talk about these things because knowledge is power and knowing the truth will set us free. People perish for lack of knowledge so it's important, especially in these times, that we get educated in racial matters for such knowledge is liberating.

A PLACE OF REFUGE

I want to delve into the concept that Africa is a Kingdom

refuge rather than a dark continent. Let's go back to Adam in Genesis 3 where God metes out judgment after the Fall to the serpent, the woman, and Adam. In Genesis 3:15 we're told that the Lord said He would put enmity between Himself and the woman, between the serpent's seed and her seed. He promised the seed of the woman would bruise the serpent's head, while the serpent would bruise His heel.

That means one thing: there would be war between them both. This prediction was fulfilled when Jesus was "bruised," when His flesh endured the crucifixion leading to death on the cross. However, it was through His death on the cross that He completely conquered the kingdom of darkness—crushing its head. He earned leadership and control over the powers of darkness. That's what was meant by Him bruising of the head of the serpent.

Going further in Genesis, we read something about a blessing. We know that Adam lost God's blessing because of his disobedience, receiving an eviction notice from the Garden. After the Flood as described in chapter 9, it says God blessed Noah and his sons but in an unusual way. God promised that all the sons of Noah were to be blessed and emerge after the destruction of the entire human race through the flood.

Of course, that meant that all the human race would trace its history from the sons of Noah. The same blessing God had declared on Adam He also declared on Noah and his sons. He blessed them to be fruitful and multiply. At that point, *all* of the children of Noah were blessed and Africa would have been included in that blessing. Africa is not a castoff or rejected continent, but a blessed continent with blessed people.

In Genesis 12, there is a development of what I see as Africa's blessing that contributed to the continent being a refuge and not a dark continent. Genesis 12:10 states there was a famine in the land so Abraham went down to Egypt to live because it was quite severe. In so doing, God used Africa to preserve Abraham in Egypt. Abraham was part of God's Kingdom purpose from whom all nations and generations would be blessed and when he was in trouble, God used Africa to preserve and protect him and God's purpose.

We then read in Genesis 37 to 50 the story of Joseph as he rescued all the tribes of Israel which carried out God's Kingdom purpose at that time. In that account, we read God's declaration to Jacob, the same declaration that He made to Adam and Eve, which was to be fruitful and multiply. This meant that the Kingdom of God and His purposes would be perpetuated through Israel as a nation.

This blessing was given to Jacob or Israel after he was given his new name. It was the blessing that had also been given Noah and his children and previously had been given to Adam and Eve. Joseph took refuge in Egypt as did his entire family. God was faithful to His promises and used Africa as a means to preserve His people and their spiritual inheritance.

Fast forward many centuries later to the Lord Jesus Christ when He was a boy. Jesus as a child fled to Egypt when Herod wanted to destroy the male children in Bethlehem. Again, we see Africa serving as a Kingdom refuge. Finally, in Mark 15, we see yet another case of aiding or "preserving" of God's Kingdom purpose when Simon of Cyrene helped Jesus to carry the cross. Simon originated from Cyrene, which is in northern Africa, part of Libya.

Someone has speculated that, perhaps, the wars and violence throughout Africa are the result of the enemy wanting to deal a blow to the rescue of God's kingdom and purposes that are going to be fulfilled by Africa continuing to serve as a Kingdom refuge. I'll leave that for you to think about.

In Mark 8:15, Jesus warned His disciples to beware of the yeast of the Pharisees and of Herod. Leaven is generally a symbol of the spreading nature of evil with only a few exceptions. Jesus was warning the disciples to be watchful of the leaven or influence of the kingdom of darkness as represented by Herod and his evil government along with the traditions of the Jewish state. Similarly, it is important to recognize that we are living in times when not all governments prevent the spread of evil. We have to be aware of the leaven of religion but also of the leaven of evil governments.

The reason I bring this up is so we can see the divide between darkness and light. As we see that, we also see that

Africa has been a refuge for the Kingdom purposes of God through the years and generations from Abraham down to Jesus. In the context in which we live, could it be again that Africa in these last days will play a role? Could Africa potentially be the source of a large portion of the end time remnant?

The Church is declining in many parts of the traditional Western world, but the Kingdom of God is advancing by leaps and bounds in Africa. Continuing with this Kingdom refuge concept, it is possible that revival in Africa and the potential preservation of a remnant there will advance the Kingdom of God in the times ahead. We are told in Ephesians 3:10 that God's purpose is to make manifest His manifold wisdom through the Church and the Church right now is strong in Africa.

When I talk about Africa. I'm talking about both Africans in Africa and those living in the Diaspora (those who have left Africa and are living abroad). This could be the reason that Africans have been spread throughout many parts of the world in the Diaspora. I'll leave that for you to consider, but I think there is a distinct possibility this is true.

Therefore, I want to encourage all my brothers and sisters, both of African and non-African descent, not to accept the supposed truth of the past that isn't truth at all. God has used Africa, is using it, and will continue to use it for His purposes. My sense is that His purpose now is as it has always been, that Africa will serve as a refuge and sanctuary for God' people where they will nurture and broadcast the truth, and many, both in and out of Africa, will be blessed because of its God-given role.

9

HE IS OUR PEACE PART ONE

Let's begin a prolonged look into the book of Habakkuk and determine what it means, according to the prophet and other passages, that the Lord is our peace. As you can read in Habakkuk 1, the prophet had a complaint about the crisis of injustice and his burden to see justice occur. When he talked to God, God told him He was going to use the Babylonians, an enemy of the people of God, to punish His people.

That gave Habakkuk another complaint so he asked the Lord how He could do that? Habakkuk set himself up in a watchtower and declared, "I'm going to hear what God has got to say about this matter." It was then that God gave him a vision for the future, part of which is found in 2:4 along with a verse we are quite familiar with in 3:17-18:

> "Behold the proud, His soul is not upright in him;
> But the just shall live by his faith" (2:4).

> "Though the fig tree may not blossom, nor fruit be on the vines; Though the labor of the olive may fail, and the fields yield no food; Though the flock may be cut off from the fold, And there be no herd in the stalls—yet I will rejoice in the Lord, I will joy in the God of my salvation" (3:17-18, NKJV).

The point is that the prophet found peace and consolation in the midst of pain, confusion, complaint, or trouble when he heard from God. He got a new song in the midst of his turmoil. We will get peace in same way in our troubling times. God is our peace if we can find Him in those times. That brings us to the book of John 14:1-2, 27:

> (1) "Let not your heart be troubled; you believe in God, believe also in Me. (2) In My Father's house are many mansions; if it were not so, I would have told you. I go to prepare a place for you. (27) Peace I leave with you. My peace I give to you; not as the world gives do I give to you. Let not your heart be troubled, neither let it be afraid."

IT IS WELL

It reminds me of a song born out of a tragic situation, *It Is Well with My Soul.* The song was written by Horatio Spafford, a young lawyer who had moved from New York to Chicago where he established his business. In 1871, he lost his firstborn son to pneumonia. As if that wasn't enough, within the same year, he lost his business through fire, although he quickly recovered. In 1873 he sent his wife and children across the Atlantic. They were meant to go together, but he remained behind to attend to business.

On the fourth day of the journey on 21 November, their vessel collided with another ship. As a result, his children perished at sea but somehow the wife survived. She was found floating and was transported to Cardiff, Wales. She sent a telegram to her husband with this line, "Saved alone. What shall I do now?" That telegram is framed in the Library of Congress. He took the next ship to join his wife and on his journey, he reached the point where the ships had collided and he had lost his children. It's at that point that he penned the words "it is well, it is well with my soul." Those words were later put to music by his friend, Phillip Paul Bliss.

It's interesting to note that out of that tragedy can come a number of good things. the first is the "it is well." Then there's a hotel serving as children center, all birthed out of their loss. How could this family find peace in these very tragic circumstances? How could such a powerful and popular song be born out of all that? This is what we're looking at now.

Looking back to the verses from John above, Jesus had just made His triumphant entry into Jerusalem. Then He continued to prepare His disciples for His crucifixion, death, and resurrection. He told them about the future and the arrival and role of the Holy Spirit and told them they should not be worried or afraid up to chapter 16. Then in chapter 17, He uttered a long prayer for His disciples and the Church that we would be preserved and be one.

WORRY

Now the first point I want to make is that you need to worry less; in fact, you need not worry at all but trust more. Jesus said not to let your heart be troubled. In other words, don't worry. Trust in God and trust also in Jesus. This chapter provides an assurance that He is going to be well with you. He's not leaving. He's going to send the Holy Spirit. He's going to give us peace. He is our source of peace.

The peace He's promising His disciples is a gift and so the question is: How do we get that peace? The key is not to worry or be afraid. How do we avoid being afraid? We do that by trusting in God, pure and simple. As Christians, we will find that in these times, it's quite easy to lose our peace and even be depressed. It's just a fact that we need to trust God. He tells us to trust Him and rely on the words He's told us. We are not to lean on our own understanding, but to trust in Him.

Continuing to build on that brings me to Philippians 4:6-8 where Paul wrote that we are not to worry about anything. Instead, we are to pray about everything:

> Don't worry about anything; instead, pray about everything. Tell God what you need, and thank him

> for all he has done. Then you will experience God's peace, which exceeds anything we can understand. His peace will guard your hearts and minds as you live in Christ Jesus. And now, dear brothers and sisters, one final thing. Fix your thoughts on what is true, and honorable, and right, and pure, and lovely, and admirable. Think about things that are excellent and worthy of praise.

Tell God what you need and thank Him for all He has done and will do. Then you will experience God's peace, which exceeds anything you can understand. His peace will guard your heart and mind as you live in Christ Jesus.

How do we not worry and trust more? We pray. Basically, Paul was telling us to pray about everything. Don't worry about anything but pray and mix your prayers with gratitude and thanksgiving. We may read a lot of motivational books, but at the end of the day, we must find a way to quiet ourselves so we can pray. Habakkuk quieted himself, prayed, and waited on God, and God was able to speak to him. He found his peace in that situation so much so that he was able to write a song out of his prayer.

We're told in the Horatio Spafford story that when Mrs. Spafford realized they were in grave danger, about 12 minutes before, she prayed as she held the children close: "God, if it's Your will, l let these children be saved, but if it's not Your will, take them." There again, her prayer played a significant role. How do we worry less and trust more? The same way she did—through prayer.

Prayer brings us to a place of peace. God illuminates our hearts and we are able to have peace. The song says, "When peace like a river attended my way, when sorrows like sea billows roll . . . it is well with my soul." You can only say it is well when you know He is God. We can only have this kind of assurance and peace from God through prayer.

Worry is our default response as human beings but we must reset and learn a new default when we become new creations in Christ. The Bible tells us the old has passed away, the new is coming, and thus we have become new creations. We are now the children of God. The old or natural man's knee-jerk reaction is worry, but we are to reset our minds and learn a new behavior just like a computer when it is in safe mode. The Bible says we will be transformed by the renewal of our minds. So how do we have peace? We have peace through prayer. That brings us to a final word that will feed our new mindset, which is not worry but trust.

There is a wonderful verse in the book of Isaiah 26:3: "You will keep him in perfect peace whose mind is stayed on you, because he trusts in You." When you have your thoughts fixed on Him, He will keep you in perfect peace. Perfect peace is built and rests on trusting the Lord, fixing your eyes on Jesus, the author and the finisher of your faith. He is your peace. He is Jehovah Shalom. He is the Prince of peace. Fix your eyes on Him because He is your peace in the middle of any storm. We are not nearly done with this DMin so let's move on to the next lesson of how to have God's peace in the next chapter.

10

HE IS OUR PEACE PART TWO

For the second part of this message, let's look further into other aspects of what was Jesus was saying concerning the connection between trusting Him and having peace. Let's pick up again at John 14:1: "Don't let your hearts be troubled. Trust in the Lord and also trust in me." I want to reemphasize that Jesus instructed us not to be afraid. In a search of the Bible, you will find that the phrase "fear not" appears 365 times. It's as if God is saying we should not be afraid every day. "Don't be anxious" would be another way of putting it. There is something God knows about us and that is our default mode is set on panic or fear.

As human beings, we are wired to worry. However, the Bible says in Philippians 4:6-7 not to worry about anything, but rather to pray. Tell God what you need and thank Him for all He has done and is doing. Then you will experience

God's peace, which exceeds anything you can comprehend. His peace will guard your hearts as you live in Christ Jesus.

I repeat: Worry is our default operating system. God expects us to reset just like a computer. As you restart a computer and get it to reset, it refreshes. When you do that, it resets the computer to a better working condition. God tells us in His Word that we are new creations dependent on Him. We are under His care, protection, and nurture. We have to reset to that thinking.

He also tells us be transformed: "Do not be conformed but be ye transformed by the renewing of your mind" (Romans 12:2). The renewal of our minds isn't just thinking or being smarter. It isn't just psychological reorientation but it's our knowledge that it's based on faith. We know our thought patterns have to be shaped by our faith because of the fact that we are new creations in Christ Jesus. That's easier said than done, but that's how we have peace based on understanding God and our position in him. The first point I made and want to re-emphasize is we are not to worry. How do we have peace? We do not worry.

PATIENT IN SUFFERING

The second point is that we have to learn to be patient in suffering. We will go through times when nothing is happening to alleviate our pain or suffering but we must be patient. Jesus addressed this in His extended discourse from John 14 through chapter 16. He then prayed for His disciples in John 17 before His death and resurrection. John chapter 16:33 is a verse I want to focus on: "I have told you all this so that you may have peace in me".

Notice He said that our peace is in Him. We will have many trials and sorrows but we must take heart because He has overcome the world. Jesus was telling them it wasn't going to be easy for them. They would have trials, temptations, and sorrows, but they were and we are to take heart because He has overcome the world. The phrase "I have overcome the world" is crucial for us to endure and be patient.

It's because of what Jesus did 2,000 years ago that we are able to overcome the world. We don't overcome the world by our might or intelligence. We will overcome the world because Jesus Christ overcame the world, and we are in Him. That's the emphasis in point two of learning how to be patient in suffering.

This is where the Holy Spirit comes to help us. Remember, two aspects of the fruit of the Holy Spirit are patience and self-control, which relate to long-suffering and being able to endure and stand strong in times of trial. As Christians, we will be tried. Proverbs 17:3 says, "There is a crucible for silver, and a furnace for gold." That means the stronger or more intense the purification, the greater the value of the end result. Gold is tried in a fiery furnace with a much greater heat than other metal but it has the highest value. That means the greater the work, the greater the calling and the more significant the assignment. There is a principle in finance and investment that the greater the risk, the greater the return. The investments that have the greater risk usually yield higher returns.

Jesus said, "Take heart, because my grace is sufficient for you." It reminds me of the gospel of Isaiah in the Old Testament. Jesus was saying through Isaiah 53:5 that "I was wounded for your transgressions." Jesus has already born the pain, endured the wounds, borne our transgressions. He was bruised for our iniquity, the chastisement for our peace was upon him, and by His stripes we were healed. That chapter in Isaiah begins by asking the questions, "Whose report will we believe?"

So, the question comes to you: What is God telling you? In this time of the pandemic, it would appear that we are going through difficult times. How do we keep our peace? Our peace is kept by our eyes being fixed on Jesus and being patient. In the Old Testament when the children of Israel were crossing the Red Sea, Moses told them, "Stand still and see the salvation of the Lord."

In other words, he told them and tells us there's a time to stop panicking and worrying. We need to stop for a moment and let our eyes look at what God can do. We need to look at the salvation of the Lord and the Word of God so we are reminded of what God can do.

What is Jesus saying? He's saying that He overcame the world 2,000 years ago. The Bible then advises us to look unto Jesus, the author and finisher of our faith (see Hebrews 12:1-2). This is the reason He went to the cross so we could have peace and healing. There is even healing for the COVID-19. There is healing in this period of pandemic. There is healing in Jesus Christ. We can look to Jesus. There are people who are going to get healed (and have been healed) because they are looking to Jesus knowing that He heals. They know that it's by His stripes that we were healed.

PPH TEST

The question then is: What is the purpose of these trials? Of course, the Bible answers the questions: Why is there suffering? Why would God allow this pandemic? You may be thinking, "I love Him. Why must I go through this? He is my God, my King, my Savior." Romans 5:1-5 states,

> Therefore, since we have been made right in God's sight by faith, we have peace with God because of what Jesus Christ our Lord has done for us. Because of our faith, Christ has brought us into this place of undeserved privilege where we know we will stand. We confidently and joyfully look forward to sharing God's grace. We can rejoice that whenever we encounter problems and trials, we know they come to help us develop endurance, and endurance develops strength of character, and character strengthens our confident hope of salvation. This hope will not lead to disappointment. For we know how dearly God loves us, because he has given us the Holy Spirit to fill our hearts with his love.

We are told to rejoice when we run into problems and trials because they will develop endurance and character, and character strengthens our hope. Why does God allow pain? He allows it to build us and strengthen our character as we endure temptations to take matters into our own hands to cut the process short. We also have more empathy for others who are going through their trials so we can strengthen and encourage them.

You will have many trials. Things may not change but the Word says, "We have peace with God." God promises we will have peace in our hearts so we aren't to worry. We are to look to Him and we will find peace. While we are going through all we're going through, our character is being renewed and built. We develop integrity and trustworthiness for our faithfulness is not based on circumstances but rather on faith. In a sense, we become battle-hardened veterans who can face difficult times with hope and lead others.

As we go through these trials in the crucible or furnace, perseverance and endurance are required. Trials are what I call character tests. In Australia, the immigration system has a Form 80, which is called a character test in immigration policy and parlance. The character test helps determine whether or not the applicant has the character qualities to fit into the Australian society. Trials are a Christian's character test, their Form 80, to see if they qualify for the Kingdom.

I have developed and look to see if disciples of Christ can pass what I call a PPH test. The first P stands for pressure, problems, pain, or troubles—all those things we experience when we are serving our Lord. That is the first element of our PPH test. The character test in the Lord is that we passed through the first P—withstand the pain while staying righteous.

The second P stands for patience, perseverance, or endurance. As we pass into the second P, God goes with us. God helps us build our endurance and perseverance which then develops character. Sometimes there is a period of time during which we feel like there is no answer from God. Sometimes there is a period of great pain and it requires perseverance for us to continue through it. We are promised that perseverance will strengthen us and produce hope which is the last of the PPH test. Simply put, hope is confident assurance. Character produces hope and confident assurance.

In my experience, we have many people in our churches who have gone through these PPH tests. At the same time, there are some who are exposed to some slight or a little pain in church or in their marriage who cannot withstand it.

They're not patient. When things seem to be going haywire, they jump out of the ship. When things go out of control, I know they are going through a PPH test to see if they are fit for the Kingdom.

People who get through the PPH can withstand pressure. People who pass the tests are able to endure and maintain their peace in a tumultuous time. This is a sign of their maturity. Pain and trials produce maturity in a Christian walk. We learn we can withstand. We can stand and aren't thrown by every wind of doctrine or season of pain. How do we do that? We know and rely on the word of God.

Jesus said a wise man is one who looks into the Word of God and obeys it. He is like a man who builds his home on a firm foundation. Winds and storms will come. We are in a time of trouble right now because of the pandemic. We were or are in pain right now, but when we are in these circumstances, we must put our confidence in God. When we pass through these trials and we are able to endure, we can then cross over to the other side. We have passed the PPH test—the pain, patience or perseverance, and hope test.

It's especially important for leaders to pass the PPH test. Have they gone through pain? What kind of problems have they endured, and have they persevered through those circumstances? Have they matured? How did they handle the pain? In my experience, people who have gone through pain have looked to the Scripture, and have passed through it with perseverance. They know how things work in God and are mature. They are developed and are useful, effective, and beneficial to the body of Christ. They give out more than they take in.

God is using the pain and developing our personal patience and our character to help us mature. As we mature, we won't be tossed by every wind of doctrine or aggravated by small things. That is how we will learn to conquer even bigger things. We have to pass through the wilderness. The children of Israel passed through the wilderness as a way of preparation for conquest. It prepared them to take the land where they were to take on the giants. They were going to take over the land which required character strength, so they would not be frightened when they encountered their enemies. It required them to overlook the little things, the little irritations.

THE CHURCH ON TRIAL

One of the things I've wondered in this period of the pandemic is if the church is on trial. I have concluded that it is. We can talk about the new normal, social distancing, masks, all of it. We have seen all sorts of things. We've seen bars being permitted to remain open, while churches could not.

Our church meets in a community hall as our church venue. We followed through with all the protocols making sure it was cleaned, limiting the number of people, ensuring that social distancing was practiced—all of it. We were going to be limited to 20 people because of our spacing issues. When we were about to resume, we went back to stage four. Then the person from the Community Council of the City Hall clearly told me that we were last on the list of preference to open because we were a church. In other words, any other organization would be able to open before the church. That seemed to be the narrative.

People can point to the conspiracy theories for the reason that the church is not a priority. That happened not only in Australia but in many other places. Something is wrong with that thinking. If a bar has priority over a church, then it also means that society has changed its priorities from where they once were. The culture and society are no longer aligned with God's priorities. Ultimately, they all will be held accountable. The earth and the governments on it are answerable to God. My question comes back to whether those governments have put the Church on trial.

Let me give you some reasons why I believe the church is on trial. I'm not questioning that the pandemic is real but some of the measures addressing that pandemic were and are dubious. For example. I have questioned the disallowed use of chloroquine. As I explained earlier, I grew up knowing a bit about medicine. I know that chloroquine has a major component named quinine sulfite. I've taken that medicine many times. When I go to the hospital here in Australia, I have to declare my allergies as all patients do and I declare my allergy to quinine.

I used to be a medical dispenser from grades two through six and I was trained to administer medicine to my fellow students. We offered hydroxychloroquine and I remember the dosages we recommended. There were no side effects. It was not dangerous, as we are now being told it is. As a scientist today, these public health measures that are being taken are highly questionable.

There is no doubt that some people are being paid to produce medical opinions consistent with certain political inclinations. There needs to be more openness as to who is behind the research for some of the studies and results that are being used to formulate public policy. We are subjected to work from people who are probably being influenced to produce certain predetermined results. I know of one such study that purports to show the dangers of hydroxychloroquine. That study is fake. Because of things like that, we have a right and need to question the results as well as who is producing them.

But the question remains: Is the Church on trial? Let me give you a few Scriptures to see how the Word of God describes or looks at the public health measures being proposed, especially where they impact the Church. Some people are saying we're going to be in these pandemic measures for a long time during which time there will be no gathering for churches. What do we say to that?

In Hebrews 10:25, we're told not to abandon or neglect the gathering together amongst ourselves. There is no gathering among believers on Zoom. Being on Zoom as a pastor is not the same as a physical meeting and cannot replace it. The Bible encourages us to gather together even as the day of the Lord draws nigh. We are meant to come together as believers. Somebody said the 120 people who were waiting for the infilling of the Holy Spirit in the Upper Room did not tarry together on Zoom. They were waiting together in one place, in one accord.

When we don't gather, we are missing out on fellowship

which is critically important. *Koinonia,* the Greek word for fellowship, is important to who we are as Christians. It seems, however, that this dynamic is going to be challenged as we move forward in this new normal of the pandemic as we face the admonition of Hebrews 10:25: "And let us not neglect our meeting together, as some people do, but encourage one another, especially now that the day of his return is drawing near."

The Bible says in Mark 16:18 that believers will lay hands on the sick and they shall recover. This is a command. There's no laying on of hands on Zoom so that means either that verse remains in effect or that verse is ignored. We have to work through this and identify what remains in place.

I see a situation where there will be a head-on collision between the Scriptures and the statutes and regulations that are being put in place because of the pandemic. There are many, many other verses that address the nature of the Church, which is to gather. What about singing in church? Psalm 96:1 says to sing unto the Lord a new song. We are not going to be able to sing. In fact, we are told that singing is a dangerous thing to do under the new regulations, but drinking in a bar is not.

You're not going to be able to sing, which is contradictory to what the Bible says. The Bible says to make a joyful noise unto the Lord. Pandemic regulations say we can't shout. Shout to the Lord and make a joyful noise under the Lord, with the voice of triumph as directed in Psalm 95:1, 98:4, and Psalm 101.

I've shown here that the Church is on trial with the new normal some are prescribing and predicting. Maybe it is time to go home, but this is *not* a time to fear for a Christian. This is what I'm saying. This is a time to look up, for when we see these things, our salvation draws near. We know the Lord is about to come back. Maranatha, even so, Lord come. He is our hope.

And that is the next thing our peace is built upon: hope. John 14:2 says, "In my father's house are many mansions if it were not so, I would have told you. I go to prepare a place for you." This is exciting. We have peace beyond the pandemic because we have hope, an eternal hope. We have to figure out where the church belongs. Maybe it's time for Jesus to come. The point is we can have peace through it all because we have an eternal hope that is beyond the grave. That hope and peace are in the person of Jesus Christ.

We see this in the Bible in the name Jehovah Shalom. Jesus is the Prince of Peace. Our peace is in the person of the Lord Jesus Christ. He states that He has overcome and we share in the victory of this with Him. We have eternal life because He has conquered death. He's the Son of God who gave Himself for us. He dwells in us through the power of the Spirit. He's our strength and peace. He's our power. As the song says, "When peace like a river attends my soul, when sorrows like sea billows roll, whatever my lot, thou has taught me to say it is well. It is well with my soul." It is well with my soul because He's my peace. He's my Jehovah Shalom.

11

THE REMNANT PART 1

In earlier chapters, I referred to the term *remnant*, which is a people of God who endure and remain to carry out His will. In this prophetic message, I will capture yet another important subject about moving forward during and after the pandemic. This is a one in a series of words of encouragement about what God is saying during this pandemic period. These messages come both to comfort and encourage us prophetically, but these chapters also contain cautions and warnings along with instructions. The word of God comes to warn us so we can take precautions.

In this chapter, I will talk more about the remnant—who they are and their purpose. We obviously sense that God is doing something unusual in this time. I want to look at not just this time, but also the time beyond this pandemic. We're eventually going to move out of this pandemic and we're going to see that this season is only one of many seasons that come to pass.

What happens after this season is important. Every season, including the season of the pandemic, is part of God's purpose. We know that the enemy intends all this and more for evil. There's an evil agenda in this period, and we are not oblivious to it. We see that the enemies of old, the Babylonians or Ninevites, came to destroy God's people, but God had a purpose and agenda in their coming. I want to emphasize that the agenda of God will come to pass. What the enemy meant for evil, as Joseph said to his brothers, God meant for good.

When times are moving forward, there's a possibility of something else being left behind. A good example of being left behind is Lot's wife. God was taking them out of Sodom and Gomorrah but Lot's wife looked back, and she missed being rescued. She became a pillar of salt. In the same way, we can miss what God is doing as we move into the next season or not be part of that next season because we tarry in the previous one. However, the remnant are the ones who are able to successfully transition into the next season.

The reality is that this season will leave some casualties. Some people will be left behind. There are people who are going to lose their salvation; others will not remain Christian. People are not meeting together and that's the end of church life for them because they have no link to the body of Christ. They don't know that church is the body of Christ, and they aren't connected. Unfortunately, people are going to just give themselves to their careers, their hobbies, or entertainment and leisure.

THE REMNANT EXPLAINED

On Sunday, the 30th of July 2020, I delivered a message to my church, the first portion of which identified who the remnant is and why I call it a remnant. Let me just begin by asking who are the remnant now? The word *remnant* is obviously an English word and it means a small part, a member of a trace remaining. God's remnant is a group of survivors. When the Jews were going through the desert, not everyone made it through. Only a small number did but all the older people who were above age 20 disappeared and died in the desert. Only the remnant went with Caleb and Joshua into the Promised Land. I can see what I call the remnant spirit among the survivors. Joshua and Caleb certainly had the remnant spirit.

The remnant carries on the work of God through a catastrophe or negative circumstances. As we're going to see, to be part of this remnant is a choice. It isn't just a group God selected, but rather it's a group purely comprised of volunteers, empowered by God's grace who have chosen to endure and be faithful. God chooses, but who does He choose? We play a role in His choice because of the positions that we must accept to be a part of that remnant.

Why is there only a remnant left? Let's again focus on Isaiah 1:9: "Unless the Lord of hosts had left unto us a very small remnant, we should have been as Sodom, and we should have been like unto Gomorrah." Isaiah talked about the remnant more than once and it's a progressive concept within the Old Testament. In the New Testament, the disciples were a remnant. Jesus fed many thousands but then when He spoke of the need to eat His flesh and drink His blood, many withdrew from Him—but not the apostles (see John 6:66-68). The people who received the Holy Spirit were the 120 people who were waiting in the Upper Room on the day of Pentecost. Those are the kinds of people who are part of the remnant I'm discussing.

In the book of Revelation 12:11, we see "They overcame the devil with the word, with the blood of the lamb, and the word of their testimony." Those are people who did not deny the Lord or give up. They were the ones who loved not their own lives unto death. Those are the remnant. To go forward, we're going to need a remnant.

Isaiah 1:9 states, "Unless the Lord of hosts had left to us a very small remnant, we would've come like Sodom and Gomorrah." In other words, the heritage of Israel would have disappeared. The Lord will leave or preserve a remnant for Himself that will carry His will and Kingdom agenda forward. The enemy always intends evil purposes, but God has His purpose in place and it will prevail.

Pastor William McDowell of Deeper Fellowship Church in Orlando, Florida preached a message in which he made an important observation I want to repeat. The remnant are made up of people who are chosen which is where the catch is for they are chosen because they choose God. They are chosen because they make decisions that honor the Lord during a time of divine visitation or divine judgment. We are in a such a place and time of divine visitation. The remnant makes decisions, and are chosen based on those decisions. God will always have a remnant.

There are two other references or examples of the remnant in the Old Testament. One is when Elijah was running away from Jezebel. He wanted to kill himself because he claimed she had killed all the prophets, and he was the only one left. God told him he was wrong because He had reserved 7,000 in Israel, all whose knees had not bowed to or whose mouth had not kissed the god Baal. God always preserves for himself a remnant. The question is: Will you be among them?

HEZEKIAH

The second example is found in a passage that is quite long so let me give you a synopsis. It's found from 2 Kings 18:1 to 2 Kings 19:37 and is a story involving King Hezekiah. The goal in this passage is for us to see the elements among the remnant that distinguished them from the others. What were their qualities? What things did they endure, what did they do that allowed God to choose them? We then want to apply those answers and insights into understanding what will distinguish a remnant in this day and age. Now to summarize the story.

We find the king of Syria attacking the city of Samaria and setting up a siege against it. Three years later, during the reign of Hezekiah, Samaria actually falls. Samaria was the capital of the Northern Kingdom, made up of the ten tribes who had rebelled against Solomon's son. The Southern Kingdom was made up of the tribes of Judah and Benjamin where Hezekiah reigned. After their conquest, the Israelites were exiled to Assyria and placed there in colonies. Why? Because they had refused to listen to the Lord their God and obey Him. Instead, they violated His covenant and the laws of Moses and so Israel had to forfeit the Northern Kingdom.

A few years later Sennacherib, king of Assyria, attacked and invaded Judah, the Southern Kingdom. He conquered their fortified cities and then came to lay siege to Jerusalem. He wanted to take over and reign in Jerusalem. Before doing that, he sent a message to King Hezekiah through three people: Eliakim the son of Hilkiah, Shebna the scribe, and Joash the son of Asaph the secretary who went out to meet Sennacherib's messengers. The attacking king basically said, "I'm coming for you."

Hezekiah offered to send a tribute to him even though he had resisted doing so previously, trying to appease him and avert the disaster of being overrun by the Assyrians. Sennacherib wasn't at all interested. In the account, however, we read how God came to rescue Hezekiah and He did so because Hezekiah represented the remnant of Israel.

There is one key aspect of Hezekiah's life that distinguishes him as a remnant and set him apart from the rest of Israel and that is his intimacy with God. He chose intimacy with God and developed a close relationship with Him. That can be broken down further into six specific expressions or character traits I would like to discuss.

The first one is righteous living. You can find evidence for that in 18:3: "He did what was right and pleasing in the Lord's sight." He made a choice and followed in the footsteps of his ancestor, King David. David was called and is remembered as a "man after God's heart." That is how he distinguished himself.

Hezekiah made a choice to follow in David's footsteps. Hezekiah's father was a terrible king and his grandfather was even more wicked. They did many wrong things but Hezekiah made a choice and that choice distinguished him from his predecessors and qualified him as a remnant. Now we know as Christians, we are the righteousness of Christ. Jesus became sin so we might become the righteousness of God, but right living is a choice we have to make.

We know righteousness exalts a nation, but sin is a

reproach to any people. Israel was suffering because of unrighteousness, having followed and worshiped foreign gods. In contrast, we see God intervening and showing up for Hezekiah, the man of God because he made righteous choices. The remnant simply decide they are going to do what is right regardless of the cost or the forces arrayed against them. No matter what, they don't get entangled or enmeshed in worldly system or lifestyle. They decide to be people with a distinction. They are not defiled.

If you remember those 7,000 prophets, God testified about them to Elijah that they had not defiled themselves with Baal. They had not bowed to Jezebel or Ahab. There is an expression we normally use in counseling, and that is to be an ally of God and those 7,000 were allies. Hezekiah was also an ally of God. Righteous living is basically being an ally of God and he was on God's side.

In the Cold War of the last century, some countries were allies aligned with America while the Warsaw Pact allies were aligned with the USSR. They made decisions in what they believed were their best interests to serve one side or the other. It is time for you to decide with whom you will establish alliances. Will you be friends with the world or God? Whatever you do and in whatever decisions you make, I urge you to be an ally of God. Be righteous. To be an ally of God is to align yourself with God's will and intentionally align yourself with the word of God. That is a choice.

POWER OF PRAYER

The second aspect of Hezekiah that made him part of the remnant was the power of prayer. In 2 Kings 19:14, we read how after Hezekiah received the letter from the messengers and read it, he went up to the Lord's temple and spread it out before the Lord where he prayed a prayer. Hezekiah was in a tumultuous time, but what did he choose to do? He made a choice to pray.

He put his hands on the letter and bowed down. I'm sure he laid himself prostrate and prayed a powerful prayer. He cried to the Lord and made a choice to seek God. As a king, one would have summoned troops or tried to get the people prepared for war. However, he didn't do that—at least not right away. That's not the only time he did that. When God told him through Isaiah the prophet that he was going to die, Hezekiah went before the Lord and prayed. He prayed and saw the Lord (see Isaiah 38:1-22). God healed him.

We see that Hezekiah was a man characterized by prayer and crying to God. The remnant pray. Theirs is a life of prayer. They seek God in calamity. The Bible says, "If my people that are called by my name shall humble themselves and pray and seek my face and turn from their wicked ways, then will I hear from them" (2 Chronicles 7:14). The remnant know the power of prayer.

In this pandemic, leaders of the world looked for a vaccine as the ultimate solution to protect lives, and that is important. However, the vaccine and other medical remedies should not undermine the need for prayer in times of calamity. God calls His people to prayer as the ultimate response during this and other periods of hardship and difficulty.

The third point that distinguished Hezekiah and qualified him for remnant status is that he removed and put away idols. We read in chapter 18:4,

> He removed the pagan shrines, smashed the sacred pillars, and cut down the Asherah poles. He broke up the bronze serpent that Moses had made because the people of Israel had been offering sacrifices to it.

The bronze serpent was named Nehushtan. Moses had been told to make a bronze serpent and put it on a pole. Whoever looked at it was saved when there was an active plague. It's interesting that the people then turned it into an idol, transforming something God used into something they used for their own purposes. They were worshiping the blessing, just like we sometimes worship our blessings. It's easy enough to do.

I speak to people in the Diaspora who prayed, and God blessed them by giving them opportunities and blessings. But how is it that some of them take their opportunity and make it into a god? That happens when they start to serve the opportunity. They've forgotten the One who brought them the opportunity. That can happen all too easily.

King Hezekiah removed idols, anything that had replaced God. We know Matthew 6:24 says that you cannot serve God and mammon. You know that in your heart there's only room for one person and that is our God. Today's idols are not wooden. Anything can be an idol, including money, family, and even family needs. Idols can be a rational and intellectual discourse. It can be the celebrity status of movie stars or even preachers.

God will not have another person or thing in His place. God will not share His worship with anyone or anything. What or who are your idols? You need to address that and tear them down. The point is that the remnant recognize, address, and tear down idols. Joshua told the people to choose between serving God and idols and made a bold statement in Joshua 24:15: "As for me and my house, we will serve the Lord."

UNWAVERING TRUST IN GOD

The fourth characteristic is unwavering trust in God. In 18:5, Hezekiah trusted in the Lord, the God of Israel. King Sennacherib asked him if he was trusting only in God. He was mocking him for doing so. The enemy always comes to question the level or quality of our trust. He puts us in a position where we aren't sure if we should trust or are trusting. That was the temptation in the garden of Eden. Will God do it? That is a question the serpent asked and it was one of who they trusted. Hezekiah had unwavering trust in God, even when conditions were dire. When conditions were bad, he still chose to trust and seek God.

Trials and torment often curtail our trust in God. This COVID pandemic is real, but our God is real and He's powerful. I'm not insinuating that COVID is not real. I'm saying He is God Almighty, the Creator of heaven and earth and the universe. This virus is tough, but God is above these things. God is able to take us through. God will rescue us at our time of need.

The attacking king mocked Hezekiah. "Can God really save you? Can prayer help you?" This COVID attack has created a lot of fearmongering. There are Christians warning everyone, "Let's be careful." Let's not forget, even for one moment, that He is the God of the universe. God rules. He's a God in heaven who never tires, and He doesn't slumber. He is in control even in a pandemic.

FAITHFULNESS AND OBEDIENCE

The fifth trait is that Hezekiah was faithful and obedient. He remained faithful to the Lord in everything. He carefully obeyed all the commands the Lord had given Moses. He was faithful which means he was dedicated, committed, consistent, constant, devoted, and loyal. As you read those words, they are words that are becoming rare. Take commitment for example.

People can't seem to stay committed to much of anything, even marriage or relationships. They can't be committed to God. However, the remnant are committed and loyal and dedicated. They're consistent in terms of priorities. If you want to know people's commitment, look at their priorities. Faithfulness is about having priorities and following them in good and bad times.

People say they have no time to be committed to a church. If people have no time for Bible study, no time for this, no time for that, they are mistaken. It's not that there is no time, it's that whatever they are not doing is not very important for them.

The question now is if your faithfulness is being tested. Can you be faithful with only online services and no physical meetings? Can you still be faithful to your church? Can you still be faithful to the time that you've set aside for church or worship? Can you be in church, or is it tea time? Is it time for church or going to work to get more hours? These answers will define your faithfulness. That's why faithfulness is being tested.

The remnant will remain faithful and be there when God wants them. Can you give money in this time when even giving is being tested? Can you give an offering without the basket being passed in church? Are you still giving your tithes and offerings in the difficult times? The remnant remain faithful even in times of hardship. I've seen people who can't be in church, but are still giving faithfully and regularly. They are giving online. Their giving hasn't changed simply because there's a pandemic. In fact, for some of them, their giving has increased because they're relying on God in the pandemic.

Here's another question to ask. Can you pray on your own? Faithfulness means that you can do things without supervision or being reminded to do them. You can be relied on to do things without being pushed or prodded to do those things.

The sixth and final point is Hezekiah was humble and repentant. The humble heart of a repentant person the Lord will not turn away. We find in 2 Kings 19:1 that when King Hezekiah heard their report, he tore his clothes, put on sackcloth, and went into the temple of the Lord. In the Old Testament, putting on sackcloth and tearing of clothes were signs of repentance. We also read in verse 14 that when King Hezekiah sent the message, he was remorseful saying, "If I have done wrong, I will repay it in tribute money. I will pay whatever money you demand." This is a state of his heart. It was repentant, just like David's was.

David had a repentant heart. Scripture calls it a repentant heart and God says He will not ignore that. When he was confronted with sin, Hezekiah repented, like his father, his grandfather, and great-grandfather did. David did not have a sense of entitlement concerning what he had. He had a humble heart and was broken before God. He did not engage in self-justification for what he had done.

Self-justification is common among some people these days in the church. They say, "I'm this way because of this problem or because of how I was raised." The explanations as to why they can't change run the full gamut of excuses. "I'm this, I'm that, I was hurt, I was abused, I had this trouble. I had that trouble." All this represents a lack of humility. A humble and repentant heart breaks easily and there is no self-justification. All those six points are related to one important practice and that is intimacy with God which is what distinguishes the remnant. Let's continue our DMin of the remnant in the next chapter.

12

THE REMNANT PART 2

Let's continue our look at the fact that God always has a remnant in every generation, men and women who have chosen to go all in and do His will—standing for Him at the risk of their own lives. I am using Hezekiah, one of the kings of Judah, as a focal point. But in this chapter, we will also look at Nahum and Habakkuk. The Bible tells us that in the last days men shall gather themselves together with itching ears to hear what they want to hear. The Church is to be a prophetic voice that declares God's unchanging truth. We believe that God speaks to us today and that we can hear him today. If you hear something that may be uncomfortable, don't close your heart. Don't tune it out because God is speaking, and we need to listen.

The pandemic showed the church everywhere that we are in need of revival and restoration. We are anticipating the next move of God. We need to anticipate what comes when we are beyond the pandemic. The remnant helps birth and usher in revival and restoration.

Throughout the pandemic, people kept referring to the new normal. We are not going back to the normal with which we had become familiar. We are going into a shift of what God intends to do. Every time there's been a downturn or challenge for the people of God, there is a season of restoration that follows. However, this restoration does not take us to the former place. Instead, it takes us to another level. It takes you to another place. It doesn't restore the former things but uses present things as the foundation for future things. It creates a new paradigm whose foundation is the purpose of God for the next generation.

It's important we realize that the remnants are part of the work of God so He can bring about His purposes on earth. Hezekiah represented the remnant at a time when there was a downturn. Things were not looking very good for Hezekiah. The remnant is such because they choose God. They choose not to bow to any other god. They choose God alone. When they choose Him, God selects and separates them to fulfill His purposes.

I predict that the times of superheroes is coming to an end so that only the Church will be recognized—not personalities but *the* personality of the Lord Jesus Christ. The Bible says that Jesus will build His church and the gates of hell will not prevail against it. God does not want anything or anyone to be idolized—not a man of God, a book, a denomination, or a move of God. He wants to be the God of gods because He is the one and only God. He warns us that we should not serve any other God but Him.

We need to understand the journey of the remnant because they are survivors and we need to learn from them if we are going to be like them and numbered among them. They are survivors who go beyond the time of trial. The point I'm trying to make here is that your journey can qualify you to become part of that remnant. However, spiritual things can only be discerned with the help of the Spirit by those who want to discern.

Look around and see that many believers are fatigued.

They are tired of COVID, and lockdowns and news. Now that we are emerging (we think), I feel like something is happening in the Spirit. I feel a move in the Spirit like in the Bible with Elijah. We need to prepare because rain is coming after a long drought. Go and prepare because I hear the sound of an abundance of rain. Rain is coming.

As I've shared previously, the remnant value intimacy with God. We are going to look at knowledge and understanding and wisdom and how they are valued as important traits of the remnant. They describe the most important characteristics or qualities of the remnant. As we read the Scripture, I encourage you to open your ears so that God's word can speak to your heart. Don't wait for the preacher to deliver the word. You can hear the word of God in Scripture as it's being read. Let's look at 2 Kings 18:1-19:37. We're not going to read every verse.

> Hezekiah son of Ahaz began to rule over Judah in the third year of King Hoshea's reign in Israel. He was twenty-five years old when he became king, and he reigned in Jerusalem twenty-nine years. His mother was Abijah, the daughter of Zechariah. He did what was pleasing in the Lord's sight, just as his ancestor David had done. He removed the pagan shrines, smashed the sacred pillars, and cut down the Asherah poles. He broke up the bronze serpent that Moses had made, because the people of Israel had been offering sacrifices to it. The bronze serpent was called Nehushtan (2 Kings 18:1-4).

Notice that the children of Israel had made what God had used to bless them in the past into an idol. The serpent was hung on a pole and whoever looked at the pole was healed when there was the plague of scorpions. What God had used to bless and save them, they turned into an idol. The same happens today. It can be a job or your family. God has blessed you with a family but then you idolize your family instead of worshiping Him. He gave you the job to provide for you, but now you give your job what you should only give to God. God is warning us against idols. God will not share our allegiance, not with your beauty or intellect or entertainment or money. He is either God or He is nothing in our lives. He doesn't want to share His glory with anything.

> Hezekiah trusted in the Lord, the God of Israel. There was no one like him among all the kings of Judah, either before or after his time. He remained faithful to the Lord in everything, and he carefully obeyed all the commands the Lord had given Moses. So the Lord was with him, and Hezekiah was successful in everything he did. He revolted against the king of Assyria and refused to pay him tribute. He also conquered the Philistines as far distant as Gaza and its territory, from their smallest outpost to their largest walled city.
>
> During the fourth year of Hezekiah's reign, which was the seventh year of King Hoshea's reign in Israel, King Shalmaneser of Assyria attacked the city of Samaria and began a siege against it. Three years later, during the sixth year of King Hezekiah's reign and the ninth year of King Hoshea's reign in Israel, Samaria fell. At that time the king of Assyria exiled the Israelites to Assyria and placed them in colonies in Halah, along the banks of the Habor River in Gozan, and in the cities of the Medes. For they refused to listen to the Lord their God and obey him. Instead, they violated his covenant—all the laws that Moses the Lord's servant had commanded them to obey. In the fourteenth year of King Hezekiah's reign, King Sennacherib of Assyria came to attack the fortified towns of Judah and conquered them. King Hezekiah sent this message to the king of Assyria at Lachish: "I have done wrong. I will pay whatever tribute money you demand if you will only withdraw." The king of Assyria then demanded a settlement of more than eleven tons of silver and one ton of gold" (2 Kings 18:5-14).

If you are a Bible scholar, you know that this is considered the First Exile and occurred around 700 B.C. Notice it is clearly stated in verse 12 that the children of Israel did not listen to God, and because they did not listen, God allowed a bad situation to come upon them because they had violated the covenant of God.

Any time the covenant of God is violated, God is violated—and that brings on calamity. It attracts evil, creates bad conditions and can lead to catastrophic results. For Israel it was very obvious but they still ignored it. They knew every time they went against the covenant of God calamity came upon them. God would judge them. They were captives for 70 years until they came to their senses and acknowledged their sin. Then their captivity ended.

Proverbs 14:34 states, "Godliness makes a nation great, but sin is a disgrace. Righteousness exalts a nation, but sin is a reproach to any people." Shame, disgrace, ruin, and destruction are the consequences when people move away from God.

> To gather this amount, King Hezekiah used all the silver stored in the Temple of the LORD and in the palace treasury. Hezekiah even stripped the gold from the doors of the LORD's Temple and from the doorposts he had overlaid with gold, and he gave it all to the Assyrian king (2 Kings 18:15-16).

Hezekiah was frightened. He was afraid and fearful reactions are usually quite predictable. We'll do what we can. He even stripped the gold from the Lord's temple just to try and appease this evil king.

> Nevertheless, the king of Assyria sent his commander in chief, his field commander, and his chief of staff from Lachish with a huge army to confront King Hezekiah in Jerusalem. The Assyrians took up a position beside the aqueduct that feeds water into the upper pool, near the road leading to the field where cloth is washed. They summoned King Hezekiah, but the king sent these officials to meet with them: Eliakim son of Hilkiah, the palace administrator; Shebna the court secretary; and Joah son of Asaph, the royal historian (2 Kings 18:17-18).

These were his go-to men who had wisdom and

experience. He sent his elite and knowledgeable men in his place. We'll see that that's important as we go along.

> When King Hezekiah heard their report, he tore his clothes and put on sackcloth and went into the Temple of the Lord. And he sent Eliakim who is in charge of the household, Shebna the court secretary, and the leading priests, all dressed in sackcloth, to the prophet Isaiah son of Amoz (2 Kings 19:1-2).

Let me contrast Hezekiah as the remnant with wicked King Ahab. When Ahab was attacked by the Moabites, he sent a plea for help to Jehoshaphat, the king of Judah. Hezekiah's reaction was very different. Like his ancestor David, Hezekiah inquired of the Lord. Let's jump to verses later in the chapter.

> And it came to pass on a certain night that the angel of the Lord went out and killed in the camp of the Assyrians one hundred and eighty-five thousand; and when people arose early in the morning, there were the corpses—all dead. So Sennacherib king of Assyria departed and went away, returned home, and remained at Nineveh. Now it came to pass, as he was worshiping in the temple of Nisroch his god, that his sons Adrammelech and Sharezer struck him down with the sword (2 Kings 19:35-37)

There were 185,000 dead! Most armies have 20,000, 30,000, or maybe even 40,000 but 185,000 men were killed by the angel of God. What a tragic end that represented for Sennacherib—killed by the sword at the hands of his sons.

I have gone into some detail about how the remnant value intimacy with God. Let me go over it again because it is important history for you to understand. Samaria or the Northern Kingdom had already been taken captive. The Northern Kingdom was made up of the ten tribes of Israel, except Benjamin and Judah. Years later, King Hezekiah was attacked. Sennacherib sent a message to Hezekiah demanding tons of gold and silver. Hezekiah was fearful and took the silver and gold from the Temple hoping to gather and pay the ransom demanded by the King of Assyria.

Look at what fear can do. Hezekiah did what he could but take notice that evil is never satisfied. It did not satisfy the evil intent of Sennacherib. Hezekiah sent for Isaiah because he knew he needed to hear what God was saying. He knew that God had a word for him and the nation. God has a word for you in this time of the pandemic and its aftermath. What is God saying? What does everybody else say? We're being bombarded by information, but the remnant hears from God.

Judah was under attack, but there was still a remnant. The remnant will always carry the word of God. What does it say in 19:31? "For out of Jerusalem shall go a remnant, and those who escape from Mount Zion. The zeal of the Lord of hosts will do this."

What are the characteristics of the remnant? The remnant value intimacy with God. They have a close relationship with God. Hezekiah valued and had a close relationship with God. He did the right thing in the eyes of God. He followed after Him. There was no one like him in Judah before or after. Why? Hezekiah chose righteousness.

Righteousness is a choice. We are the righteousness of God in Jesus. Jesus saves us now because our righteousness is like filthy rags before God. When we are saved, God expects us to walk in the light. He expects us to walk in righteousness. Righteousness is a choice. With the help of the Holy Spirit, we walk that path of righteousness. God helps us to walk that path of righteousness and that qualifies us to be part of the remnant.

We see that Hezekiah depended upon God through prayer. He put away the idols. He pulled down the Asherah. He tore down the shrines. He restored the worship of Jehovah God. The Word in John 4 says that the time has come when God seeks worshipers who will worship Him in spirit and truth. They don't worship in any other fashion. They don't venerate anything apart from God. They worship the Lord alone. They don't consume worship. They produce worship.

The remnant chooses God instead of convenience. The remnant is distinct and not politically correct. It's not the politically correct who will inherit the Kingdom of God, but only the righteous will gain the inheritance. You must choose to be different. The remnant will choose persecution rather than bowing down to false gods.

Look at Shadrach, Meshack, and Abednego. They chose not to bow down. Our God is able to preserve us. Even if He does not rescue us during this pandemic, we will not bow down. Our God is able! We need to decide not to bow, because through that decision God will rescue us. The remnant is chosen because they choose God.

The remnant trust God. In 18:5, it says, "Hezekiah trusted in the Lord God of Israel, so that after him was none like him among all the kings of Judah, nor who were before him." He's not just another God. He's not just one option for worship. He is the God of the universe. He's the God of Israel. He is the God Adonai. He's the God Yahweh. All power belongs to him. Hezekiah had an unwavering trust in God even when the conditions were dire. When the conditions were threatening, Hezekiah chose to believe God.

If you look at the text, you find that there was intidimidation. "Can this god save you? Have they heard what the Assyrians do? This is not a joke what the Assyrians do to their enemies. They can consume you. Can your God really save you?" The enemy intimidates through fear mongering. You hear the rumors. "Look at what they did to the Northern Kingdom. Look at what happened in Samaria."

Remember the story of the lepers at the gate in 2 Kings 7:3-20? People were eating donkey's dung because their enemies had surrounded them. However, I choose to follow the example of David. In the time of calamity, David said, "Don't worry, King Saul. Goliath, this uncircumcised Philistine, will be delivered into my hand" (my paraphrase). God will deliver us out of the pandemic. We have a God who is all-powerful and beyond the Coronavirus. Our God is a God of the upper hand.

Trust says "I will faithfully take the challenge head on." Trust says "I will face that which is in front of me." Trust says "He rescued me yesterday, He can do it again today. I have seen His arm rescue me before. This is not going to be difficult for

Him. I have seen Him heal cancer. I have seen Him heal my headache. I have seen Him heal my backache. He is able to do it again. He is going to do it again."

David trusted his God. David told Goliath, "You come at me with a sword and the spear and a javelin, but I come to you in the name of the Lord of Heaven's armies, the God of the armies of Israel whom you have defied today. Goliath, the Lord will conquer you" (my paraphrase). Today we say, "COVID, you come to me with the sophistication of a virus. You come to me with all the scientific explanations. However, we serve a God of good news."

Do you remember what Nahum said? "How lovely upon the mountains are the feet of him who brings good news. I will sing peace proclaiming news of happiness. Our God reigns" (Nahum 1:5). We have a God who is on the throne. We have a God who cannot be defeated. Dysfunction cannot scare God. Poverty cannot scare God. All power belongs to God. Hezekiah had this kind of trust in God: "He remained faithful to the LORD in everything, and he carefully obeyed all the commands the LORD had given Moses" (2 Kings 18:6).

You see the contrast between Hezekiah and Judah and the children of Israel in the North? The northern tribes decided to disobey God. They decided to take the bronze idol and worship it. They decided not to worship the true God. On the other hand, Hezekiah chose to obey the Lord and the commands He had given to Moses. He was faithful and obedient. Faithful means he was committed, a commitment that was rare then and now.

Hezekiah decided to be committed to his God. Commitment is loyalty. Commitment is devotion. I'm not talking about Facebook kind of loyalty. It's not about friending and unfriending. It's not following and un-following or a blocking type of commitment and loyalty. Commitment means that there is a priority and an affection of the heart.

One of the rules I have in the classes I teach is that if I get a call from my wife or my children, I'll answer it. I do that because I'm committed to my wife and children. My commitment to them is greater than my commitment to my class and my students. They are a higher priority than my class.

Part of commitment is faithfulness. The Bible says we are required to be faithful to our God. That's the kind of faithfulness God is looking for when He returns. The Bible says that He is looking for the faithful on earth (see Luke 18). The problem is that we see faithfulness diminishing and dwindling—except among the remnant. All we have to do is look around and see the lack of commitment and faithfulness. Hezekiah was faithful to God, however, in good times and in bad.

Is the Church being faithful in the time of this pandemic and the days following? Our faithfulness is being tested. Faithfulness means consistency in doing what we say we are going to do. Daniel was faithful in his commitment to God. At 3 p.m., he prayed every day regardless of what the prime minister said. His priorities did not change. Many times, because of convenience or hardship, our priorities change.

I saw a newspaper cartoon that advertised for "light church." It was poking fun at the low level or lack of commitment in today's church. Two-point sermons instead of a three. We've reduced the millennium to only 800 years. We no longer have Ten Commandments, just eight. Sadly, many would be attracted to that kind of church.

Another article said that 90% of the parishes across the country require less commitment than a Kiwanis Club. Faithfulness is not about what you and I want. Faithfulness is about what God wants. What does God require of us at this time? He requires faithfulness. Faithfulness is what you do when nobody is looking. It's about your relationship with God.

Christianity in some places today is about show. It's about how many times you appear before somebody else. You know when you're being faithful as much as you know when you're not being faithful. The Bible says that even if we are unfaithful, God cannot be unfaithful because He cannot be unfaithful to Himself. Hezekiah chose what was pleasing to God and that made him the remnant.

The other element of this is intimacy with God. Chapter

19:1 states, "When King Hezekiah heard their report, he tore his clothes and put on sackcloth and went into the Temple of the Lord." Hezekiah went before the Lord with the letter from Sennacherib and spread it out before Him. Hezekiah humbled himself before the Lord. The word says God resists the proud and gives grace to the humble. The God of the universe will come against you if you are proud. Pride comes before destruction. God will come against you.

Pride says, "I'm okay even though I'm walking in sin. I'm not walking right but neither is anybody else so I'm okay." That's the pride God comes against. Humility is not having a sense of entitlement: "You owe me this. You owe me this position. You owe me this respect." There is a sense of entitlement that has crept into the Church and it is rampant.

There are times when people offer analytical explanations as to why something can or can't happen. We can find excuses for everything. "I was abused as a child so I can behave the way I'm behaving." I understand that people have diseases but there are people who use disease as an excuse for bad behavior. I'm not making light of people with valid issues, but there are many people who have their "reasons" for their behavior. These reasons are nothing more than excuses.

There are many who, despite their conditions, despite their circumstances, despite their hardships, trust God for their deliverance. If God doesn't deliver you, God can help you, and He will give you the grace you need to endure and go through. Humility does not hide behind anything. The Bible says that God sees the broken heart and a broken and contrite heart He will not despise. God is looking for the humble in heart so He can lift them up. The remnant is humble and broken before God. God will respond to prayer, to humility, and to brokenness.

Hezekiah was humble and broken before God. He laid out the letter and had on sackcloth. Sackcloth represents humility and repentance. He tore his clothes, symbolizing a rending of his heart before God in brokenness. God is on your side. Joshua said, "Choose you this day whom you will serve. As for me and my house, we will choose the Lord." Who are you going to serve? Choose who you're going to serve because God is looking for the remnant He can count on and use. The remnant chooses Him. He will choose them and set them aside for Himself. He will use them for His glory.

God answers prayer. It may seem like He takes a while, but God is quick to act and slow to anger. As truly as the sun rises in the east and sets in the west, God is coming through for His people—including you. The question is: Will you choose God? The remnant always chooses God. Here's an example of another remnant:

> Then the Lord appeared to Solomon by night and said to him: "I have heard your prayer and have chosen this place for Myself as a house of sacrifice. When I shut up heaven and there is no rain, or command the locusts to devour the land, or send pestilence among My people, if My people who are called by My name will humble themselves, and pray and seek My face, and turn from their wicked ways, then I will hear from heaven, and will forgive their sin and heal their land" (2 Chronicles 7:12-14).

God is restoring the land. God is restoring your situation. God is restoring the world to himself. Restoration is not about the way things were but rather leads to a better future. "Because I know the plans I have for you, plans for good and not for evil plans for her future and a hope. You will seek me, and you will find me when you seek me with all your heart. I will restore your fortunes." God is restoring. God is saying, "Choose Me." The remnant obey God. The remnant are faithful. The remnant choose God and when they choose Him, God chooses them. They will not be destroyed. When God chooses them, the nations that oppose them will be destroyed. It's because of the remnant the Church will not be judged.

Our prayer should be, "Lord, I choose You today. Lord, I seek You today. God, I recommit my way back to You. I know it is You, God, who will restore what the canker worm has eaten. You are a God who restores. I know You are about to recover all the enemy has stolen from me."

The joy that has been taken away from you, God will

restore that joy. God is a God of restoration. He is restoring what the evil one has stolen. God is going to restore the Church of Christ. God's going to restore the ministry for the glory of His name. God does not condemn. God restores. God is our strength.

He is our everything. When everything else seems to be taken away, God is our help. We can rely on God. We can put our trust in God because He never changes. In a time of lockdown and pandemic, God is our strength. We can call on His name because He hears our prayers. He is an ever-present help in our time of need, in our time of trouble. He does not change. He calls us to come to Him. He will not turn us away.

When we feel we are fallen, God is there to pick us up. When we have no hope, he is there to give us hope. We serve a God of restoration. We serve a God of restoration through resurrection power. And because of that, by His grace we can be part of His remnant. You can be part of His remnant. Let's continue to look at the important and historic role of the remnant in the next chapter as we continue to examine Hezekiah's response to crisis.

13

THE REMNANT PART 3

In this third part of our DMin concerning what I am calling the remnant, let's go back to look at other lessons we can learn from King Hezekiah. He's not only an example of the remnant, but we can contrast him with the leaders in Israel, the Northern Kingdom, when he acted as an individual and leader of faith in Judah. Hezekiah dared to be different. We will look at how that difference expressed itself.

Hezekiah started his reign as an achiever, someone who took action for righteousness sake. He eliminated idolatry which had become rampant, especially during his father's reign. We also see that King Hezekiah led a pilgrimage to Jerusalem. This happened also during his father's reign. God uses ordinary people, men of like passions, even during down times, to save nations. They are able to do so because they dare to be different.

It's important to emphasize the role ordinary people play in times of calamity and crisis. God has used people like you and me to save nations because they dared to be different. These are the people I'm referring to as the remnant, people who dare to be different when all others are conforming out of fear.

THREE ELEMENTS OF THE REMNANT

There are three elements I see in Hezekiah's life that made him part of the remnant: intimacy with God, knowledge, and valuing the knowledge one has. Let's start by reading from 2 Kings 18:

> During the fourth year of Hezekiah's reign, which was the seventh year of King Hoshea's reign in Israel, King Shalmaneser of Assyria attacked the city of Samaria and began a siege against it. Three years later, during the sixth year of King Hezekiah's reign and the ninth year of King Hoshea's reign in Israel, Samaria fell. At that time the king of Assyria exiled the Israelites to Assyria and placed them in colonies in Halah, along the banks of the Habor River in Gozan, and in the cities of the Medes. For they refused to listen to the Lord their God and obey him. Instead, they violated his covenant—all the laws that Moses the Lord's servant had commanded them to obey.
>
> In the fourteenth year of King Hezekiah's reign, King Sennacherib of Assyria came to attack the fortified towns of Judah and conquered them. King Hezekiah sent this message to the king of Assyria at Lachish: "I have done wrong. I will pay whatever tribute money you demand if you will only withdraw." The king of Assyria then demanded a settlement of more than eleven tons of silver and one ton of gold. To gather this amount, King Hezekiah used all the silver stored in the Temple of the Lord and in the palace treasury. Hezekiah even stripped the gold from the doors of the Lord's Temple and from the doorposts he had overlaid with gold, and he gave it all to the Assyrian king. Nevertheless, the king of

> Assyria sent his commander in chief, his field commander, and his chief of staff from Lachish with a huge army to confront King Hezekiah in Jerusalem. The Assyrians took up a position beside the aqueduct that feeds water into the upper pool, near the road leading to the field where cloth is washed. They summoned King Hezekiah, but the king sent these officials to meet with them: Eliakim son of Hilkiah, the palace administrator; Shebna the court secretary; and Joah son of Asaph, the royal historian (2 Kings 18:13-18).

Then we continue into 2 Kings 19:

> When King Hezekiah heard their report, he tore his clothes and put on burlap and went into the Temple of the Lord. 2 And he sent Eliakim the palace administrator, Shebna the court secretary, and the leading priests, all dressed in burlap, to the prophet Isaiah son of Amoz (2 Kings 19:1-2).
>
> That night the angel of the Lord went out to the Assyrian camp and killed 185,000 Assyrian soldiers. When the surviving Assyrians woke up the next morning, they found corpses everywhere. Then King Sennacherib of Assyria broke camp and returned to his own land. He went home to his capital of Nineveh and stayed there. One day while he was worshiping in the temple of his god Nisroch, his sons Adrammelech and Sharezer killed him with their swords. They then escaped to the land of Ararat, and another son, Esarhaddon, became the next king of Assyria (2 Kings 19:35-37).

Let me summarize what we have just read. The Northern Kingdom of Israel had fallen, and the King Sennacherib of Assyria came to attack Judah. His chief messenger delivered a message demanding Judah's unconditional surrender and of course, the first responses of the leaders and people were fear and panic. Hezekiah tried to appease the king, but it didn't work.

In chapter 19 we see a totally different response because Hezekiah did not fear, but instead went to the house of God to seek the Lord. The remnant value knowledge, which is exactly what Hezekiah did. When I refer to knowledge, I'm talking about accurate information. I'm talking about making sure that the facts and figures are correct. Beyond that is the second level, which is understanding. Understanding is interpreting the facts beyond the surface to get at the exact meaning of that knowledge. The remnant go deeper than just the surface of what it appears to be.

The first level of knowledge is information. How did Hezekiah seek information? How did that appear in Hezekiah's action response? In 2 Kings 18:18, they summoned King Hezekiah, but the king sent these officials to meet with them: Eliakim son of Hilkiah, the palace administrator; Shebna the court secretary; and Joah son of Asaph, the royal historian.

This information gathering strategy of Hezekiah was demonstrated through the composition of the team of people he sent. They were knowledgeable and wise in their roles within the kingdom, people of high standing. The second group he sent was different. He wanted a good assessment of the situation from a wide variety of people. That is a characteristic of a good leader. He sends people who are able to investigate and can provide him with accurate information.

The response of those he sent was sensible and levelheaded. Meanwhile, Hezekiah had pulled the gold overlay off the doorways which showed a sense of panic. He was concerned as to what was going to happen. He recognized there was a big army on the horizon. We read later how many came and how many remained but it all painted a picture of a ruthless enemy capable of a skilled attack by experienced warriors.

When we get information like Hezekiah received, our first instinct is fear, a normal reaction. We too may start taking the gold off our doors, so to speak. If you look in the context of the pandemic, there is a lot of information out there through the mainstream media. What's the importance of numbers daily reporting of infections? The initial response is to fear, terror even. Hezekiah displayed a similar reaction at first. He was afraid. It's a surface level response to getting information and accepting it at face value. There's another verse I want to read. Hosea 4:6 is written in about the same period of time:

> "My people are being destroyed because they don't know me. Since you priests refuse to know me, I refuse to recognize you as my priests. Since you have forgotten the laws of your God, I will forget to bless your children. My people are being destroyed because they don't know me. God's people are destroyed here because of lack of knowledge."

This means that the remnant will not be destroyed when others are being destroyed like the Northern Kingdom was. The remnant with Hezekiah in the Southern Kingdom were saved because of the truth of the word of God. Hezekiah accurately represented and carried out that truth. The Word tells us that Jesus said we will know the truth and the truth will set us free (see John 8:32).

God's exhorted His people in Hosea to have knowledge, but the knowledge He wanted them to have and hold on to was from His word. Joshua had said centuries before Hosea that the law should not depart from their mouths: "You shall meditate on it day and night and you will succeed in all you shall do" (Joshua 1:8). The knowledge of the Word is knowledge of God. That's level one knowledge: information.

Wisdom is level two knowledge. "What God of any nation has ever been able to save its people from my power? So, what makes you think the Lord can rescue Jerusalem from me?" The people were silent and did not utter a word, because Hezekiah had commanded them not to answer him. The king's messenger was mocking God and Hezekiah but the people did not say a word.

That's sometimes good advice: Don't talk too much. Sometimes it's actually necessary to keep quiet, especially when you're under enemy attack. That was the case there. They didn't need to talk and give more incentive to the enemy. It's wise not to say anything. The Scriptures tell us to be still and see the salvation of the Lord (see Exodus 14:13).

Here's another illustration of the wisdom and knowledge of God. There is wisdom in knowing that God will act, and that God will be our rescuer. A keyword which I relate to both wisdom and understanding is revelation. Revelation is being able to see or uncover truth below the surface. Another important word here relevant to the remnant is discernment. Discernment is being able to test and then identify the spirits. In Deuteronomy 4:6, Moses spoke to the children of Israel:

> "Therefore, keep and do them [the statutes of God], for this is your wisdom and your understanding in the sight of those nations. We shall hear all these statutes and say surely this great nation is a wise and understanding people."

Moses was encouraging the children of Israel that the word of the Lord they received would become their understanding and their wisdom. That indicates there is the wisdom of this world and the wisdom of God. Moses was telling the children of Israel that the wisdom of God would come from the word of God. The Word of God is a revelatory word.

When we have a good relationship with God, then we have wisdom, and there is revelation. The book of James said that whoever doesn't have wisdom should ask God and He won't hold back their request (James 1:6, my paraphrase). The word also tells us that the best of man's wisdom is foolishness in God's eyes.

I'll give you another illustration of a man who did the wrong thing using the wisdom of man and that was Abraham. Sarah suggested that Abraham takes her handmaiden Hagar and be intimate with her so they could have a son. That turned out to be disastrous because it was the wisdom of man, producing results that were not in line with God's plan or will.

There is wisdom in waiting on God, which Abraham and Sarah did not exhibit. That is what we learn from this story in the word of God. Hezekiah, on the other hand, had wisdom: "Be still and see the salvation of God." In Isaiah 30:15 we read, "In quiet confidence shall be your strength." There will be strength found in one's quiet confidence in God.

UNDERSTANDING

The third level of knowledge is understanding. In 2 Kings 19 we read,

> After Hezekiah received the letter from the messengers and read it, he went up to the Lord's Temple and spread it out before the Lord. And Hezekiah prayed this prayer before the Lord (2 Kings 19:14-15).

The first response of fear was natural and normal but in his second instance, Hezekiah realized that this was all beyond his ability to handle it. He understood that he was involved in a spiritual and not natural war. We know he realized it was spiritual warfare because his reaction addressed the spiritual perspective of the situation. His engagement with the problem took on a spiritual nature and he looked for a spiritual response. He had the knowledge and wisdom led him to gain an accurate understanding or perspective of the entire scenario. He went to the house of the Lord and that is where he recognized the nation was at spiritual war.

Let me once again apply this insight to the pandemic we are in. What is happening now? There is a spiritual aspect of this. On the surface we see the natural, but there is a greater spiritual dimension. The remnant understands this and sees beneath the surface which is usually only the tip of the iceberg. The remnant will be able to understand that and go deeper. If we don't understand what's going on spiritually, then we will miss the most important point.

Notice that Hezekiah spread the letter out before the Lord. To me this is symbolic of taking it to God. There's the old song that advises us to take it to Jesus. "Are you sad? Do you have troubles? Take it to Jesus?" What did Hezekiah do? He took his troubles to God. Whenever he did that, he got understanding.

That is always the result of effective prayer. Through prayer we are able to understand. We don't just pray or pray only with our spirit but also with our understanding. How do we pray with understanding? We pray with understanding when we seek and obtain a revelation. It's important that we grasp what we are told in second Corinthians:

> The weapons of our warfare are not carnal but mighty in God in the pulling down of strongholds. Casting down arguments and every high thing that raises its head against the knowledge of God, bringing every thought into the captivity to the obedience of Christ, being ready to banish all disobedience when the obedience is fulfilled (2 Corinthians 10:3-4).

When we understand that we are in spiritual warfare, then we are able to engage and use our weapons that are not carnal. Hezekiah entered into spiritual warfare without him firing or the enemy firing one single arrow at Jerusalem. Hezekiah was able to engage in the war on a spiritual level.

He did this because of his trust in the Lord, his belief in God and his faithfulness to engage the unseen dimensions that constitute a spiritual battle. We see that when there is moral decadence, falling standards, God out of schools, and abortion, the people are avoiding Kingdom purposes and principles. In fact, righteousness and the righteous are mocked.

The enemy of our souls, the god of this world, hates God's Kingdom purposes for the Earth. That scares Satan to hell. But Jesus says, "I have overcome the world. Be of good cheer" (see John 16:33). Jesus also said "I will build my church and the gates of hell will not prevail against it" (Matthew 16:18). In spiritual warfare, the Lord would have us know that the battle belongs to Him. This is an important message I want to pass on to you through a variety of verses. The first is in 2 Kings 19:20-21:

> "Then Isaiah son of Amoz sent this message to Hezekiah: 'This is what the Lord, the God of Israel, says: 'I have heard your prayer about King Sennacherib of Assyria.' And the Lord has spoken this word against him: 'The virgin daughter of Zion despises you and laughs at you. The daughter of Jerusalem shakes her head in derision as you flee.'"

There are two things I want to emphasize in those verses. The first is that God hears and answers the prayers of His people. That was the message to Hezekiah: God has heard his prayer. God answers prayer. You don't have to worry about enemy attacks because God answers prayer.

The second thing we learn from Hezekiah is that the enemy you see will flee and he will be chased by the allies you cannot see. In another version, it says, "You will see the backs of your enemy because they will flee." In another passage, Moses and the children of Israel were told that they would no longer see the Egyptians. In other words, there were going to be victory and an answer to prayer.

In 2 Kings 19:28, a strong message of encouragement and exhortation came out of this whole situation: "Because of your raging against me and your arrogance, which I have heard for myself, I will put my hook in your nose and my bit in your mouth. I will make you return by the same road on which you came." This was exciting news for God promised to deal with the Assyrian enemy on behalf of His people. Their enemy was God's enemy because they were attacking God's people and mocking them.

Notice that He said they would return the same way they came. That was powerful, exciting, and encouraging for those who heard it. The remnant stand with God and choose God and because they do, God chooses to fight on their behalf. God restores and rescues on their behalf because of the remnant. We read another part of the message in verses 32-34:

> "And this is what the Lord says about the king of Assyria: 'His armies will not enter Jerusalem. They will not even shoot an arrow at it. They will not march outside its gates with their shields nor build banks of earth against its walls. The king will return to his own country by the same road on which he came. He will not enter the city, says the Lord, for my own honor and for the sake of my servant David, I will defend the city and protect it.'"

Let me break this down further for you. God promised to defend Jerusalem. God will defend His purpose and Jerusalem was part of His Kingdom purpose. He said that not even one arrow would be shot at His people. Notice He also said, "for the sake of my servant David."

God remembered and emphasized the covenant nature of His concern. If God can do that with His servant David through that covenant, what do you think He will do with the covenant He made through the blood of HIs own Son, the son of David, Jesus Christ of Nazareth? May you be encouraged with the fact that God honors and defends His covenant.

ACROSS THE GENERATIONS

I want to also point out that His protection and coverage are cross-generational. The covenant was made with Hezekiah, but it had already existed for generations. We hear about generational curses, but we also should know that there are generational blessings. The children of the remnant will be blessed. There's a generation of younger ones that will be raised up. I'm seeing my sons and my son's sons, and they are going to be on fire for the Lord. This is part of my generational blessings.

The next generation will be stronger in the Lord. The remnant out of this situation will be a powerful army that He will raise up. Ezekiel asked if those dry bones could live. We find the response in Ezekiel 37, "Out of those dry bones, a great mighty army is rising up" (see Ezekiel 37:3-6).

Out of this pandemic, a great and mighty company of people is rising up to become the army of God. Revival is taking place because the remnant carry the anointing of God. Second Kings 19:30-31 then had this to say about the remnant:

> "And you who are left in Judah, who have escaped the ravages of the siege will put roots down in your own soil and will grow up and flourish. for remnant of my people will spread out from Jerusalem, a group of survivors from Mount Zion, the passionate commitment of the Lord of heaven's armies will make this happen."

The remnant of the house of Judah shall again take root with their roots going downward and their fruit growing upward. That is a great promise! The fortunes of God's kingdom and God's purpose will be restored. There will be fruit.

For just as out of Jerusalem would go a remnant, out of

COVID will also be a remnant. There's a remnant that always emerges during a downturn in history. Any time there's been a calamity and it looks as if the people of God are finished, there have been revival and restoration. The remnant emerge and are commissioned to carry on the mission and to fulfill God's purpose on earth. The remnant become those that carry on the mission of God's restoration.

This is never about you or your enemy. As a child of God, you are part of the Church of God. It's never about individuals. It's always about the purpose of the Kingdom of God. It's not about the darkness, it's about God's Kingdom purposes. It's not just about the humans, but also about God's purpose that the enemy is trying to destroy.

The enemies of God's people are God's enemies. It's a scary thing to be against the God of the universe and have Him as an enemy. Any enemy of God's people will suffer the wrath of God. God will defend His people wherever they are. Hezekiah saw 185,000 of the enemy's soldiers die in one night. That's how God rescued His people. There's always going to be a remnant and God hears their prayers. God will defend his remnant. The restoration, revival, and blessing go from one generation to the next. Hezekiah was the son of Abijah. Abijah received a generational blessing from Zachariah. The remnant are the chosen of God and will flourish in any situation, even out of a pandemic.

The remnant are the chosen of God because they choose God! Out of the calamity, the remnant are the chosen of God. I'm tearful as I finish this chapter, I know that God will rescue His people. God will secure that which is His. Jesus promised that He would build His church and the gates of hell, though they rise up and oppose it, shall not prevail against it.

14

THE REMNANT PART 4

Let me review what I have already shared about the remnant. The remnant value intimacy with God. We started with the point that the remnant love knowledge, of which there are three levels: information, wisdom, and then understanding. In this chapter, I'll talk about the power of relationships and present excerpts from the book of 2 Kings 18:5-6, 13 (NKJV):

> He [Hezekiah] trusted in the Lord God of Israel, so that after him was none like him among all the kings of Judah, nor who were before him... For he held fast to the Lord; he did not depart from following Him, but kept His commandments, which the Lord had commanded Moses... And in the fourteenth year of King Hezekiah, Sennacherib king of Assyria came up against all the fortified cities of Judah and took them.

Then in 2 Kings 19:1-2, we read,

> And so it was, when King Hezekiah heard it, that he tore his clothes, covered himself with sackcloth, and went into the house of the Lord. Then he sent Eliakim, who was over the household, Shebna the scribe, and the elders of the priests, covered with sackcloth, to Isaiah the prophet, the son of Amoz.

Let's examine the power that emanates from and through godly relationships. We will look at three aspects of relationships that are important, beginning with chapter 18:1-2:

> Now it came to pass in the third year of Hoshea the son of Elah, king of Israel, that Hezekiah the son of Ahaz, king of Judah, began to reign. He was twenty-five years old when he became king, and he reigned twenty-nine years in Jerusalem. His mother's name was Abijah the daughter of Zechariah.

Family relationships played an important role in the life and reign of King Hezekiah, who we have been holding up as a model of the remnant. King Hezekiah's father, Ahaz, was one of the worst kings of Judah. He reinstituted idol worship, especially the god Baal. He tore down parts of God's holy temple so he could rebuild and then worship the Asherah poles.

In contrast, Hezekiah's mother, whose name was Abijah, was the daughter of Zechariah who was a spiritual counselor to King Uzziah. We see the strong influence of his mother to do the right thing before the Lord and to follow the commandments. The Bible also restates that Hezekiah was of the lineage of King David. Through this we see the significance of his parents and the family in Hezekiah's life. Abijah was pious and righteous and presented a good example for Hezekiah. This shows us that it's time to invest in and nurture the potential of the family.

FAMILIES

During the time of being shut down in the pandemic, God has reminded us of the significance of families. When everything was shut down, we retreated to our family units. Imagine what a challenge it would be if the family wasn't the right place to be. There have been lots of battles during this time and some families have been torn apart. Moral decadence and violence in particular have especially targeted families.

There are anti-family and anti-marriage messages. Same-sex marriages, for example, do not provide for reproduction and that is not a family but they are honored as such. All that is working to undermine God's concept of the family. We see why the enemy is working to destroy the family when we see the power of strong, godly family relationships in this story.

In 2 Timothy 3, Paul wrote about the traits of people in the last days that people would be lovers of themselves, lovers of money, boastful, and scoffers against God. He also mentioned something important concerning family relationships that there would be widespread disobedience to parents. However, it's important to God's agenda that there be positive family influence across the generations. In this epistle, therefore, God is reminding us that we need to invest in building strong families. The value of family is evident in the life of Hezekiah. The remnant value those family relationships.

TRUSTED ASSOCIATES

The second point I want to point out about Hezekiah is found in 2 Kings 18:18:

> And when they had called to the king, Eliakim the son of Hilkiah, who was over the household as the palace administrator, Shebna the scribe, and Joah the son of Asaph, the royal historian came out to them.

They were in a place called Lachish and the armies of the Assyrian King Sennacherib were there. They summoned Hezekiah, but he sent out trusted men to confer with the Assyrians. This was reminiscent of David and his mighty men who were around him. In 2 Samuel 23:13-17, we read,

> During harvest time, three of the thirty chief warriors came down to David at the cave of Adullam, while a band of Philistines was encamped in the Valley of Rephaim. At that time David was in the stronghold, and the Philistine garrison was at Bethlehem. David longed for water and said, "Oh, that someone would

> get me a drink of water from the well near the gate of Bethlehem!" So the three mighty warriors broke through the Philistine lines, drew water from the well near the gate of Bethlehem and carried it back to David. But he refused to drink it; instead, he poured it out before the Lord. "Far be it from me, Lord, to do this!" he said. "Is it not the blood of men who went at the risk of their lives?" And David would not drink it. Such were the exploits of the three mighty warriors.

David's trusted men were in David's family of relationships. Similarly, we see Hezekiah also surrounding himself with trusted men. They were important in his life. He sent them ahead and they returned with valuable information.

We live in a time when there are often only shallow commitments in building relationships. God is encouraging us to reemphasize and return to the importance of relationships—and not just in families but also in one another. Did you know that your success and destiny are tied to others? Sometimes their success and destiny are tied to you.

Following this pattern of thought, we see how Hezekiah sent these three men out because of his trust in their relationship. David had his mighty men. Elijah and Elisha were in a trusted relationship. What we're talking about is having people around you who you know and can trust.

Sometimes we can be careless about and not invest in those relationships. We can let their relevance diminish, but relationships are like a bank account. If we only withdraw from a relationship and don't deposit anything into it, soon that account is bankrupt. How much are we investing in relationships? How connected are you to others?

Consider the concept of koinonia or fellowship, not only from the perspective of the physical or biological family, but also from the family of God's people. That's important as we learned from the book of Acts regarding the early Church. There we see that the believers lived together as a community of likeminded saints. They ministered one to another.

It is noted that great grace flowed amongst them. There

was power that was the foundation for the disciples' ministry. This shows us that spiritual power flows through relationships of both family and friends. The bottom line is Hezekiah had trusted people around him. It calls for commitment from all parties to develop those kinds of relationships.

Sometimes God puts us in a place or connects us with somebody. We then find we have to be committed to the cause *and* the person. A story is told about David Livingstone when he came to Africa. Friends wrote to him and said that they wanted to send him other men but were asking if he had found a good road into the area yet. David Livingstone wrote back and replied, "If the men are men who will only come if there's a good road, I don't want them. I want men who have said they will come if there's no road at all!"

Relationships require people who are willing to sacrifice and are committed to the cause, not just people who are looking for the convenience or glamour of association. Relationships grow when we are committed. It's good to have people around who know when you are hurting and help you get to your destiny. Are we consumers or producers in the area of relationships? Are we draining the relationship bank account to bankruptcy? If we contribute and produce, then the relationships will grow.

CONNECTED TO GODLY LEADERS

His third relationship (family and trusted associates were one and two) was with a servant of God. When Hezekiah heard the Assyrian chief of staff of Sennacherib King of Assyria (the Rabshakeh) mocking and deriding God's people, he sent Eliakim his scribe to Isaiah the prophet. From this incident alone we learn four lessons.

First is the question of how we should pray. The second is God's answer through the prophet, which was the prediction of the fall of Assyria and Sennacherib. The strategy came from God, indicating that the remnant always depend on God's strategy for survival. The third lesson is found in the poetic message to the enemy, the precision with which the answer from God came. There was a sad ending for Sennacherib as predicted in verse seven.

The Sovereign God outlined exactly what would happen. Accordingly, the enemy king would receive a message that would frighten him and cause him to think he needed to flee together with his troops and go home where he would be killed with the sword, ending his career. That's exactly the way it was given to Isaiah. It's obvious God was saying, "I've heard your prayer" and that He would act without delay. We read in 2 Kings 19:6b-7, 20, 34-37:

> Do not be afraid of the words which you have heard, with which the servants of the king of Assyria have blasphemed me. Surely, I will send a spirit upon him, and he shall hear a rumor and return to his own land; and I will cause him to fall by the sword in his own land. . . . Then Isaiah the son of Amoz sent to Hezekiah, saying, "Thus says the Lord God of Israel: 'Because you have prayed to Me against Sennacherib king of Assyria, I have heard. . . And it came to pass on a certain night that the angel of the Lord went out and killed in the camp of the Assyrians one hundred and eighty-five thousand; and when people arose early in the morning, there were the corpses—all dead. So Sennacherib king of Assyria departed and went away, returned home, and remained at Nineveh. Now it came to pass, as he was worshiping in the temple of Nisroch his god, that his sons Adrammelech and Sharezer struck him down with the sword.

God predicted a sad ending to Sennacherib king of Assyria in answer to Hezekiah's prayer, which demonstrates that God will hear the prayer of the remnant and respond. Indeed, God was reminding us during the pandemic of the truth found in Daniel 2:34 that we are in the season predicted through the vision given to Daniel: "You watched while a stone was cut out without hands, which struck the image on its feet of iron and clay and broke them in pieces." Matthew 21:42-44 brings clarity to the appropriate interpretation of this passage in Daniel 2 through what Jesus said: "Have you never read in the Scriptures: 'the stone which the builders rejected has become the chief cornerstone. That was the Lord's doing, and it is marvelous in our eyes.'"

It is safe to conclude that Jesus is the stone and the prediction and promise are that He will act with precision. We are living in a period of time where He will ultimately grind away and bring to an end the kingdoms of this world (see Revelations 11:15). Whether it's Nazi Germany, the Greek and Roman empires, or the Medes and Persians, we see a pattern of history where God has brought an end to the careers of kings and the greatness of countries and empires.

In the case recorded of Belteshazzar in Daniel 5, God wrote on the wall, "You've been measured in the scales and found wanting" (Daniel 5:27). God is in charge and in full control of the history of nations and humanity in general. This is in line with what the Word says that there shall be no end to His kingdom or government and the peace thereof (see Isaiah 9:7).

God will act. Whatever time it is, even in this period of the pandemic, the message to us is that God will act according to His purpose as outlined in His Word. He will hear our prayers. Hezekiah humbled himself and put on sackcloth and prayed. He prayed and God answered his prayer.

God is calling us to prayer and humility because this is how His Kingdom purpose is realized on earth. Remember the prayer in Matthew 6, "Thy kingdom come." When they pray, He speaks through his prophets. Many times, we don't hear it or perhaps it's more accurate to say, we don't recognize the prophetic voice. He will do exactly as He said He would to defend His people, to defend His Word, and to bring about His purpose and the advancement of His Kingdom on earth.

GOD SAVES HIS REMNANT

The fourth and final lesson from the encounter between Hezekiah and the Assyrian king Sennacherib is found in the message that pertained to the remnant. There was a message to the enemy but also a message to the remnant of Hezekiah. He promised that there would be devastation for two years where they could not eat their own fruit, but in the third year they would be fruitful. He promised their roots would go down and the fruit would go up. It was explained that the zeal of the Lord would do this. That is a message of hope and restoration which God always has for His people in times of calamity.

We're going to see great destinies being fulfilled in this time of difficulty. Psalm 92 promises that even in our old age, we will bear fruit. That is happening now. I want to encourage you as you read this that your purpose is not over as long as you are breathing.

Moses was at his peak age while leading the children of Israel at the age of 80. God is saying to the remnant that those who seek and choose God, God chooses them—they are His remnant. They will be fruitful just as He told Hezekiah he would be fruitful. That brings us to the last part, which is really two parts found in 2 Kings 19:32-34:

> Therefore thus says the Lord concerning the king of Assyria: "He shall not come into this city, nor shoot an arrow there, nor come before it with shield, nor build a siege mound against it. By the way that he came, by the same shall he return; and he shall not come into this city," says the Lord, "for I will defend this city, to save it for my own sake and for my servant David's sake," says the Lord.

That's powerful. He said, "I'm coming. No arrow will be shot. They will not occupy the city." Military tactics were deployed against Hezekiah that included shooting arrows, building high siege towers, occupying high ground, and strategic command posts. All these military tactics failed when God intervened and promised, "I will defend My people." Psalms 125 states,

> Those who trust in the LORD are like Mount Zion, which cannot be shaken but endures forever. As the mountains surround Jerusalem, so the LORD surrounds his people both now and forevermore. The scepter of the wicked will not remain over the land allotted to the righteous, for then the righteous might use their hands to do evil. LORD, do good to

> those who are good, to those who are upright in heart. But those who turn to crooked ways the Lord will banish with the evildoers. Peace be on Israel.

Those who trust and rely on the Lord, the remnant, are like Mount Zion which cannot be moved but remains forever. As the mountains around Jerusalem, so the Lord surrounds His people, from this time and forever. God is saying, "I will defend my people." He has promised divine deliverance and protection for His people, His remnant. Deliverance and protection are in the hands of the Lord.

In summary, God will always preserve and protect a remnant who choose to follow Him with their whole heart. When they pray, He will answer their call. Their enemy will fall and fail. God will deliver and protect His people. We've seen throughout this remnant DMin the importance of relationships in the family, the power of relationships in circles of people God has put around you, your confidantes. This includes the fellowship and the relationships among believers, the family of God.

We also looked at the importance of a connection with a man of God from whom the message of God flows. The Bible says, "Believe the word of God and you'll be established. Believe the word of the prophet, and you will succeed or prosper" (2 Chronicles 20:20). Which relationship is God telling you to mend, to invest in, or to get away from?

CONCLUDING THOUGHTS

After I finished the manuscript, I had a bit more time to study and share from Habakkuk, who we looked at in Chapter 9. I have learned more timely lessons relevant to this season of the pandemic. Let's go back to Habakkuk for a moment. The prophet was burdened and complained to God about the violence, injustice, and arguments he witnessed. In reply, God made the situation even worse by telling Habakkuk how He was going to bring judgment to Judah through an evil and vicious Gentile nation named Babylon.

Habakkuk's reaction was quite predictable. He asked God, "How can You, a gracious and loving God, do that? How can you allow such evil?" As an answer, God gave Habakkuk a vision of what He was going to do in the future. In other words, God revealed His purpose of salvation in the future in Habakkuk 2:4.

God then instructed him to write down the vision he would see. God told him of a specific time coming when the just would live by faith. Now we know He was speaking about the era of salvation through Jesus Christ. As a result. Habakkuk had peace with God and even sang a song: "I will rejoice in the Lord of my salvation" (Habakkuk 3:17).

What is the key lesson that we can learn for today from that book and the summary I've given of that and the other lessons you have just read? All these chapters and messages indicate the essence of what it means to walk with God.

Habakkuk had that kind of close walk with God, so close that he was able to carry what I see as a God-given burden concerning the state of the nation of Judah. As a result, God shared His wisdom through revelation to Habakkuk and the prophet had peace.

Psalms 2:14 says that the secret of the Lord is with those who fear him, and He will show them His covenant. In other words, God makes known His ways and reveals His secrets to the humble. Even in these difficult times of the pandemic and its aftermath, God is revealing His secrets to those who walk intimately with Him. That's why I've said throughout this book that intimacy with God is an important way enabling you to pass through these seasons. Then I pointed out that you must be humble, and if you are, then God will reveal His secrets to you.

What God told Habakkuk in the vision was to have an impact on Paul centuries later. We can read that Paul said the just shall live by faith in Romans 1:17, Galatians 3:11, and Hebrews 10:38—although there's disagreement as to who wrote Hebrews. Then much later in human history, we see the words of Habakkuk had an impact on Martin Luther in the Reformation around 1517. Those words were "the just shall live by faith." If you are just, if you want to be part of God's remnant, you must have faith.

This is my prayer in these days and I invite you to make it your prayer as well:

> *"Lord, help me to humbly have a close walk with thee, that I may learn to hear Your voice in the midst of all the voices: political, scientific, and religious arguments, to have a deeper revelation of You and Your purposes. May I declare Your oracle at the appointed time. Lord, may I hear Your voice in this time, even in the pandemic; may I speak that which I hear from You."*

The Lord bless you!
Pastor Melphon Mayaka

ABOUT THE AUTHOR

Melphon holds a Doctor of Philosophy in Management from Monash University, Australia. Until founding Uwezo Liberty, Church Melphon was an Associate and Youth Pastor at the Truelight Christian Church, a ministry of the Australian Christian Churches Melbourne (ACC) in Victoria, Australia.

Before founding Uwezo Liberty Church together with her husband, Pastor Melphon, Esther served as the women's ministry leader at her local church in Kenya called East Assembly (formally Kenya Assembly of God Buru Buru). Prior, she had also served in the worship ministry at the Christ Co-workers (CHRISCO) Fellowship in Nairobi.

Esther loves to see the family strengthened and has a heart for women and people in general. She and her husband, along with her three sons, Elijah, Joshua, and Isaac, form a formidable ministry team.

to contact Pastor Melphon, please email him at:

melphonm@gmail.com

or visit the church website at:

https://uwezolibertychurch.org

www.ingramcontent.com/pod-product-compliance
Lightning Source LLC
Chambersburg PA
CBHW072019040426
42447CB00009B/1666
* 9 7 8 1 6 3 3 6 0 1 8 7 1 *